Paradigm Shift

European Academy of Religion (EuARe) Lectures

EuARe Executive Committee:
Karla Boersma, Francesca Cadeddu, Jocelyne Cesari,
Alessandro Ferrari, Hans-Peter Grosshans,
Pantelis Kalaitzidis, Peter Petkoff,
Herman J. Selderhuis, Kristina Stoeckl

Volume 7

Paradigm Shift

Seventh Annual Conference 2024

Edited by
Herman J. Selderhuis

DE GRUYTER

ISBN 978-3-11-914387-5
e-ISBN (PDF) 978-3-11-221890-7
e-ISBN (EPUB) 978-3-11-221914-0
ISSN 2940-455X
DOI https://doi.org/10.1515/9783112218907

This work is licensed under the Creative Commons Attribution 4.0 International License. For details go to https://creativecommons.org/licenses/by/4.0/.

Library of Congress Control Number: 2025939914

Bibliographic information published by the Deutsche Nationalbibliothek
The Deutsche Nationalbibliothek lists this publication in the Deutsche Nationalbibliografie; detailed bibliographic data are available on the Internet at http://dnb.dnb.de.

© 2025 with the author(s), editing © Herman J. Selderhuis, published by Walter de Gruyter GmbH, Berlin/Boston, Genthiner Straße 13, 10785 Berlin.
This book is published with open access at www.degruyterbrill.com.

www.degruyterbrill.com

Questions about General Product Safety Regulation:
productsafety@degruyterbrill.com

Contents

Herman Selderhuis
Introduction —— 1

Alberto Melloni
History and the Story of the Religious Object —— 3

Alexander Kulik
Naming God and Other Challenges of Transcultural Monotheism —— 27

Elisabeth Gräb-Schmidt
The Anthropological Turn of Religion – Towards a Paradigm Shift in Transcendence References in Modernity —— 45

Vincent Goossaert
Gods as persons and subjects: Proposals from China for a comparative approach —— 63

Herman Selderhuis
Introduction

This 7th volume in the series EUARE LECTURES contains the four keynote lectures presented at the European Academy of Religion's Seventh Annual Conference held in Palermo, Italy, May 20–23, 2024 as it was organized by FSCIRE.

The overarching theme of the conference was "Paradigm Shifts", and four keynote speakers were invited to offer papers about the topic from their particular point of view: Prof. Alberto Melloni (University of Modena and Reggio Emilia), Prof. Alexander Kulik (The Hebrew University of Jerusalem), Prof. Elisabeth Gräb-Schmidt (Eberhard Karls University of Tübingen), and Prof. Vincent Goossaert (Ecole Pratique des Hautes Etudes). The text of these lectures is presented in this volume.

The expression "paradigm shift" can be fruitfully applied to scholarship regarding religion. It can highlight when and how the multiple disciplines of the broader field of religious studies found ways to change their own perspectives and the manner of defining, reading and analyzing the objects of their analyses. Paradigm shifts result for example from positive or conflictual engagement with major historical events, the use of innovative theoretical lenses to further understand the significance of religion, the adoption of brand new or established technologies which bring disruptive discoveries to the fore, but essentially also through the ways in which historical events or social, political and/or intellectual developments affect views on religion, religious standpoints and practices as well as research on religion.

All four presenters approached the theme from their specific area of research and demonstrated how fruitful and challenging paradigm shifts can work, but also how a forced shift in paradigm can lead to overlooking fundamental aspects of religion and to neglecting established research. Key element in these lectures is the question how the paradigm shift caused by the anthropological turn in religion affects the relevance of religion and of theology and religious studies for other academic disciplines as well as for politics and society. This element touches the mission of the European Academy of Religion as an academic forum promoting research, increasing academic quality and creating awareness for the role of religion in the public square.

Herman Selderhuis, President European Academy of Religion

∿ Open Access. © 2025 the author(s), published by De Gruyter. This work is licensed under the Creative Commons Attribution 4.0 International License.
https://doi.org/10.1515/9783112218907-001

Alberto Melloni
History and the Story of the Religious Object

In these pages I will propose some theses on the object of historical-religious re-search drawing from my own limited and specific scholarly work. I do not say this in order to, *ante tempus*, supply some autobiographical relic of *ego-histoire*,[1] nor to circumvent Niklas Luhmann's brocard about the uselessness of explications,[2] but simply to demarcate my point of observation.[3]

Having applied myself to the study of Christianity, most often in its Western and Roman Catholic form, focusing on its sources and institutions, I have made my own the postulate that Christianity has always – and can only – move within his-tory. This has always obliged it to take nourishment (by emulation, by competition, by contamination, by mutation, by contrast) from a historically determined rela-tionship with the cultures and "religions," *latu sensu*, that it "has come in contact with."[4]

I am well aware that to know religion is to know none. But compared to the dispute between Max Müller and Adolf von Harnack in the late 19th century from

---

1 See Pierre Nora, ed., *Essais d'ego-histoire* (Paris: Gallimard, 1987); Anna Cole, "'The History That Has Made You,' Ego-Histoire, Autobiography, and Postcolonial History," *Life Writing* 16 (2019): 527–538.
2 That is: "If someone needs this to understand what I have written, then I have written poorly," ("wenn jemand das braucht, um zu verstehen, was ich geschrieben habe, dann habe ich schlecht geschrieben"), Walter van Rossum and Niklas Luhmann, "Ich nehme mal Marx," in *Niklas Luh-mann: Archimedes und wir: Interviews*, ed. Dirk Baecker and Georg Stanitzek (Berlin: Merve Verlag, 1987), 14–37. On this, see Detlef Pollack, "Niklas Luhmann: Funktion der Religion (1977)," in *Schlüs-selwerke der Religionssoziologie: Veröffentlichungen der Sektion Religionssoziologie der Deutschen Gesellschaft für Soziologie*, ed. Christel Gärtner and Gert Pickel (Wiesbaden: Springer VS, 2019), 322–333.
3 I have benefited from the way Étienne Fouilloux, *Au cœur du XXe siècle religieux* (Paris: Éditions Ouvrières, 1993), expressed the indispensable instances (clarifying the relationship between re-searchers and subject, demanding a comparative history, establishing the link between religious and global history, building a truly complete religious history) within his path of research.
4 This expression is part of the statutes of FSCIRE (Foundation for Religious Studies) drafted in 1985 by Giuseppe Alberigo and available at fscire.it. On that institute's trajectory, see Giuseppe Alberigo, *L'"officina bolognese" 1953–2003* (Bologna: EDB, 2003). An examination of cultural expres-sions of religion can be found in my recent work, Alberto Melloni, "The Greatness and Misery of Interfaith Dialogue: A Historical Critique of an Unprecedented Effort," *Studies in Interreligious Di-alogue* 32 (2022): 113–133.

Open Access. © 2025 the author(s), published by De Gruyter. This work is licensed under the Creative Commons Attribution 4.0 International License.
https://doi.org/10.1515/9783112218907-002

4 —— Alberto Melloni

which that statement came,[5] I think that the assumption may have a more radical scope today. To know religion is to know none because religions, *strictu sensu*, considered in themselves – as abstractions expressed in absolute form, or as a bookish distillation rationalized *a posteriori* – simply "do not exist."[6]

What the Eternal asks and reveals to the human condition – including the eternally absent Eternal of atheism and that which is skirted by agnostic ablation – exists only if and when someone takes on and makes the question and command their own. A religion (a faith, a belief, a moral attitude) exists only if and when someone scrutinizes foundational texts in order to make them into a rule of life or to understand those who made them. It exists if and when a canon of practices and doctrines is embraced or studied in order to understand its perceived assertiveness on those who observe it. It exists only if and when individuals and communities express rituals and ethics that have emerged from the unfathomability of consciousness to the surface of the legible.[7] Since no "religion" (which is the free adherence to a higher dutifulness[8]) is therefore ever lived in a context where there are no *other* Scriptures or other readings of the same Scriptures, no *other* rules or other normative deductions of the same patrimony, no *other* practices or doctrines or forms of worship to constitute a fabric of dialectical references,[9] to regard such faith as a detached

---

5 Often attributed to Ed Parish Sanders, the phrase comes from Friedrich Max Müller, *Einleitung in die vergleichende Religionswissenschaft* (Strasbourg: K.J. Trübner, 1876), 14; it was challenged by the famous proclamation of Adolf von Harnack, *Die Aufgabe der theologischen Fakultäten und die allgemeine Religionsgeschichte*, of August 3, 1901 in honor of the founder of the University of Berlin with the variant "Anyone who does not know this religion does not know any and anyone who knows it and its history knows all" ("Wer diese Religion nicht kennt, kennt keine, und wer sie samt ihrer Geschichte kennt alle"), which had already been expressed by Reinhard Pummer, "Religionswissenschaft or Religiology?," *Numen* 19 (1972): 91–127. For its use in the Third Quest and in its reinterpretation of Paul, see Ed P. Sanders, "Comparing Judaism and Christianity: An Academic Autobiography," in *Redefining First-Century Jewish and Christian Identities: Essays in Honor of Ed Parish Sanders*, ed. Fabian E. Udoh, Susannah Heschel, Mark Chancey, and Gregory Tatum (South Bend, IN: University of Notre Dame Press, 2008), 11–41.
6 See Melloni, "The Greatness and Misery."
7 See Pier Cesare Bori, Mohamed Haddad, and Alberto Melloni, eds., *Réformes: Comprendre et comparer les religions* (Münster: LIT, 2007). On the radical pluralism of religions, see Jean Greisch, "La religion et les religions," *Archives de Philosophie* 63 (2000): 229–246.
8 I am using a definition of my own, which I will not dwell on here. For an examination of the 20th century debate, see Giovanni Filoramo, *Che cos'è la religione: Temi, Metodi, Problemi* (Turin: Einaudi, 2004), and Robert Crawford, *What is Religion?: Introducing the Study of Religion* (London: Routledge, 2002).
9 See Pier Cesare Bori, "Ogni religione è l'unica vera: L'universalismo religioso di Simone Weil," *Filosofia e teologia* 8 (1994): 393–403, and Pier Cesare Bori, *Per un consenso etico tra le culture e Lettera sui monoteismi* (Bologna: Marietti1820, 2023).

bubble that could be placed on an autopsy table as some dead thing would deprive it of its relational and interconnected structure, which is what makes it "real" and thus graspable by the unnatural science that is historical knowledge.

This is not why I aspire or presume to be a historian "of religions." While I have the deepest respect for (almost[10]) all those who practice this discipline, I do not feel restricted from taking up another, and I refuse to feel diminished by using the historical-critical method from a more precise academic field. This is because my area of research, like many others, requires slow-accumulating knowledge, indispensable linguistic tools, fairly deep toolboxes, and a familiarity with a broad range of sources and arguments.[11] And aside from knowing that I am incapable of doing so, I do not think that there is anyone who uses other methods (those of an ethno-

---

10 The two who opted out are Einar Thomassen, former president of the network of national associations known as the European Association for the Study of Religions (EASR), and Tim Jensen, president, since 2015, of the International Association for the History of Religion (IAHR, the institution that denied membership to the American Academy of Religion because of an act that Giovanni Casadio claimed credit for). Thomassen and Jensen signed a statement in response to the founding of the European Academy of Religion (EuARe), a statement whose exquisitely ideological character seems to me at a distance of a few years even more evident and which can be documented simply by pointing out the arbitrary assertions, slanderous inferences, and inquisitorial logic of suspicion of that brief text (debunked then and later by the function EuARe has had). In their indictment, Thomassen and Jensen argued that "despite its name, we regard this Academy as not representing the non-confessionally based and globally-oriented approach that is essential to the study of religions as an academic discipline. This impression is reinforced by the published program of the Academy's first conference, [rectius: *zero conference*] to be held in Bologna on 18–22 June [2017] this year on the theme 'Research in the Religious Fields' which is strongly dominated by themes relating to Christian theology and aspirations concerning interreligious dialogue, and which hardly addresses the world of religions outside Europe and its fringes. The pursuit of normative theology and engagement in interreligious conversation are legitimate activities in their proper context, but they fall outside the generally accepted definition of the study of religions as a field of evidence-based research. (The empirical study of such activities is, naturally, a valid topic of research in the study of religions.). In conclusion, the EASR and the IAHR see this new organization, which pretends to be a comprehensive European association for religious studies, as an unfortunate initiative, taken, as it seems to us, with the intent of displacing an existing organization for the academic study of religion in Europe. We regard this enterprise as an attempt to divert the perception of the study of religion in the public sphere, as well as its sources of funding, in a direction that is detrimental to the study of religions as an academically rigorous field of research, as well as to the pursuit of unbiased knowledge about religions which is needed if the challenges of contemporary societies as well as their historical roots are to be correctly understood."

11 In this reflection, I have made a close comparison with the theses expressed by Mauro Pesce, "Alla ricerca di un nuovo schema mentale (Appunti utili anche per la linea editoriale di 'Annali di Storia dell'Esegesi' nei prossimi anni)," *Annali di storia dell'esegesi* 40 (2023): 13–40.

6 —— Alberto Melloni

anthropological comparison[12] or religious sociology[13]) or other registers (like the discursive[14] or disclosive[15] ones) that can achieve the same degree of knowledge that specialists, and others, consider their benchmark.

I put every effort into being a historian[16] who applies general tools of knowledge to a particular field, in which individual and collective work can make one seek and find another ounce of the phenotype of truth that historical truth belongs to.[17] In the face of pathetic attempts to escape fatigue and uncertainty by taking pseudo-historical shortcuts or adhering to editorial fashions that avoid the sanction of academic evaluation systems, I hold the attitude of *risum teneatis*. They do not, however, escape the scorn of those who know that – in the field of religion – to exempt oneself in that way from the rigor required by the historical-critical method is to step outside an epistemic perimeter that can never again be re-entered.

Employing that method in that sphere does what all "general" histories do, but does not accept to practice or theorize the religious-historical research as a subsector of general histories. Let me be clear, there are neither few nor fool those who

---

12 This is outlined in Lionel Obadia, "La part anthropologique du symbolisme religieux: Praxéologie, pragmatique et politique," *Archives de sciences sociales des religions* 85/143 (2009): 33–43.

13 See Danièle Hervieu-Léger, "Faut-il définir la religion? Questions préalables à la construction d'une sociologie de la modernité religieuse," *Archives des sciences sociales des religions* 63 (1987): 11–30.

14 For example, Kocku von Stuckrad, "Discursive Study of Religion: From States of the Mind to Communication and Action," *Method & Theory in the Study of Religion* 15 (2003): 255–271, who used the approach theorized by Hans G. Kippenberg, "Diskursive Religionswissenschaft: Gedanken zu einer Religionswissenschaft, die weder auf einer allgemein gültigen Definition von Religion noch auf einer Überlegenheit von Wissenschaft basiert," in *Neue Ansätze in der Religionswissenschaft*, ed. Burkhard Gladigow and Hans G. Kippenberg (Munich: Kösel, 1983), 9–28. An application to rituals in the digital world can be found in Kerstin Radde-Antweiler, *Ritual-Design im rezenten Hexendiskurs: Transfer-prozesse und Konstruktionsformen von Ritualen auf Persönlichen* (Saarbrücken: Südwestdeutscher Verlag für Hochschulschriften, 2011).

15 See Gillian Polack, "History and Fiction: Writers, their Research, Worlds, and Stories," *Spiel* 30 (2011): 73–88.

16 There are not a few in Italy who call themselves "studiosi di storia storici" ("student of history" historians in order to identify themselves with Delio Cantimori's untranslatable self-definition. On his Emilia-Romagnan story, see Giovanni Miccoli, "Delio Cantimori," in *Il contributo italiano al pensiero: Storia e politica*, ed. Giuseppe Galasso and Adriano Prosperi (Rome: Treccani, 2013), and Piero Craveri, "Delio Cantimori," in *Dizionario Biografico degli Italiani*, vol. 18, 1975 (Rome: Istituto della Enciclopedia Italiana), available at www.treccani.it/enciclopedia/delio-cantimori_(Dizionario-Biografico).

17 Here I am following Yosef Hayim Yerushalmi, on whom see David N. Myers and Alexander Kaye, eds., *The Faith of Fallen Jews: Yosef Hayim Yerushalmi and the Writing of Jewish History* (Chicago: Brandeis University Press, 2014).

always treat the same era as a sufficient extension to their inquiries and treat the religious dimension as a lens, magnifying a detail that is and remains such. This is not to say that it is acceptable to reduce religious history to a subsection of a general periodization that suffers or panders to academic power relations in the name of the right to a career. I also find unacceptable the ambitions to claim priority that are emerging from new scholarly areas (post-colonial studies, gender history), convinced that they have a right to a voice that religious history has lost.

Instead, I think that the historical knowledge produced by the many academic disciplines that traverse or are traversed by religious experience – individual or collective, material or immaterial, institutional or emotional – rightfully belongs to the family of the historical sciences by *method*, but that it has a uniqueness that lies in its *object*. It is an object identified *by and with* a structural breadth, which as a rule requires a stratification of readings, studies, analyses, and approaches that are specific and totalizing because they need to cover dilated times in a voluntary and conscious way.

The historical-religious approach is not a long-term chronicling nor one that appeals to paleontology or neurology to override the human in its individuality. It is not an approach whose segments compile "other presents" that are distant from us and autonomous from one another like the containers of an imaginary public utility cargo terminal. "Religious life" sketches a path in which each time refers back not only to the "before" that precedes it, but to an original "before" (*norma normans non normata*), a "primitive" before (that of the *ecclesia primitiva*), a "before" that rediscovers and reenacts the norm or form, or rather, refers to a "before" undone by the deformation and tampering with pre-existing conceptions.

1

The defense of the uniqueness of a specialized historical-religious history does not claim any special status for it. Like all historiography, it lives within a certain moment and is affected by the place given to history in the public paideia, in the academic system, and in the marketplace of knowledge that weaves the intellectual societal fabric.[18]

---

18 See Francesco Benigno, *La storia al tempo dell'oggi: Che cosa chiediamo alla storia?* (Bologna: il Mulino, 2024) and his earlier work, Francesco Benigno, *Words in Time: A Plea for Historical Rethinking* (London: Routledge, 2017).

8 —— Alberto Melloni

In our recent history, as is known, something has indeed happened that has touched all histories. Like it or not (and I do not), history has left the *paideia* of the ruling classes as well as the *forma mentis* of global public opinion. It has left a bit of popularization to console the widows and consumers of a culture that has retreated to narrower terrain where popularization, education, and a narcissism about one's marginality and research ambitions live alongside one another.

In the regime of modernity and the secular era – as Reinhart Koselleck's conjecture (*Vermutung*) posits through heuristic anticipation[19] – history has provided both the ruling classes and the social institutions with a repository of arguments of multiple uses and has built its own list of suppliers (of methods, lexicons, tools, and of paradigms that have become models and totems).[20] This process has come about by replacing that branch of theology called theodicy with history. After 1755, according to the philosopher Odo Marquard, the tools that theodicy gave the Almighty to answer the question *"si Deus, unde malum?"* are taken up by history, which now must justify humanity before the (historical) evil that it is capable of and must absolve individuals, peoples, and nations, sheltering them from eternal or changing moralism in order to make their freedom safe.[21]

To carry out this operation of/on history, modernity elected a venue (the Humboldtian-type university which welds teaching and research together), defined a sphere (the past and those who have been its subject), elected a method (the study of sources), recognized a benchmark (Ranke's famous *eigentlich/wirklich*[22]), and

---

19 On the "heuristic anticipation" (*heuristischer Vorgriff*) that assumes the 18th century turn from its effects, see the latest essays by Reinhard Koselleck, *Begriffsgeschichten: Studien zur Semantik und Pragmatik der politischen und sozialen Sprache* (Frankfurt a.M.: Suhrkamp, 2006), with essays by Ulrike Spee and Willibald Steinmetz, and an afterword by Carsten Dutt.

20 See the entry on "Geschichte," in *Geschichtliche Grundbegriffe: Historisches Lexikon zur politisch-sozialen Sprache in Deutschland*, ed. Otto Bruner, Werner Conze, and Reinhard Koselleck, 2nd ed. (Stuttgart: Klett-Cotta Verlag, 2004), orig. ed. 1977–1988. Also, Reinhard Koselleck, *The Practice of Conceptual History: Timing, History, Spacing Concepts*, trans. Todd Samuel Presner (Stanford: Stanford University Press, 2002), and Reinhard Koselleck, *Begriffsgeschichten, Studien zur Semantik und Pragmatik der politischen und sozialen Sprache* (Frankfurt a.M.: Suhrkamp, 2006).

21 See Odo Marquard and Alberto Melloni, *La storia che giudica, la storia che assolve* (Rome-Bari: Laterza, 2008).

22 The famous thought comes from Leopold von Ranke, *Geschichte der romanischen und germanischen Völker von 1494 bis 1535*, v. 1 (Leipzig: Duncker & Humblot, 1824), v–vi: "History has been given the office of judging the past, of instructing the world for the benefit of future years; the present attempt does not submit to such high offices. It merely wants to tell how it actually was" [the first edition has "to say how it really is"] ("Man hat der Historie das Amt, die Vergangenheit zu richten, die Mitwelt zum Nutzen zukünftiger Jahre zu belehren, beigemessen; so hoher Ämter unterwindet sich der gegenwärtige Versuch nicht. Er will bloß sagen, wie es eigentlich gewesen ist" ["sagen, wie es wirklich gewesen ist"].)

History and the Story of the Religious Object — **9**

achieved a state of consciousness, which conventionally appeals to Max Weber's definition of *Beruf* or Marc Bloch's *métiér*.[23] All of this is valid and holds both for the historian of an epoch or of a field such as the history of Christianity, or any other quadrant of the religious, from which a function that could be called "social" was expected.

For those who write and read in the regime of modernity, *historia rerum gestarum* had an active function in the *res gestae* of the present because it established a vision of the future without untangling the contradictions. History (any history) nurtured the aspirations for freedom as much as the civilizing "duty" of colonialism, explained the fate of capitalism and historical materialism, generated nationalist resentment and constitutional systems, produced and tore down regimes, explained and contested wars – on a path in which "progress"[24] constituted a contradictory compass in the intermediate steps even if its final destination were assured – at least until it was seen (a hundred years ago...) that what we call "progress" is nothing more than the accumulation of rubble at the feet of Walter Benjamin's *Angelus Novus*.[25]

That historical culture that shaped, nurtured, and provided inoculation in the face of ideologies has been replaced by a presentism (now simply uncultured, marked by the ideology of global hyper-consumerism known as globalization[26]) that has left citizenship only to two artifacts of that system of knowledge, that is, on the

---

23 See Susanne Rau, Birgit Studt, Stefan Benz, Andreas Bihrer, Jan Marco Sawilla, and Benjamin Steiner, eds., *Geschichte schreiben: Ein Quellen- und Studienhandbuch zur Historiografie (ca. 1350–1750)* (Berlin: Akademie Verlag, 2010).

24 Reinhard Koselleck, *Vergangene Zukunft: Zur Semantik geschichtlicher Zeiten* (Frankfurt a.M.: Suhrkamp, 1979).

25 On the articulation of messianism and its secularization, see Michael Löwy, *Walter Benjamin: Avertissement d'incendie, Une lecture des thèses "Sur le concept d'histoire"* (Paris: PUF, 2001), and Howard Eiland and Michael W. Jennings, *Walter Benjamin: A Critical Life* (Cambridge, MA: Harvard University Press, 2016). On the leap of discontinuity, see Irving Wohlfarth, "Smashing the Kaleidoscope: Walter Benjamin's Critique of Cultural History," in *Walter Benjamin and the Demands of History*, ed. Michael P. Steinberg (Ithaca, NY: Cornell University Press, 1996), 190–205.

26 The eclipse of history has created space for the economistic presentism that has hegemonized the *forma mentis* of the ruling classes: the culture of historicism in all its nuances has been replaced by an economic mechanism quite distinct from Marx's historical materialism.

10 —— Alberto Melloni

one hand, public history with explanatory functions of the present,[27] and, on the other, an advocacy with which to justify one's ambitions about the future.[28]

The eclipse of the *paideia* of the ruling classes from history does not mean that that type of study has taken a different path from that of the other sciences: they too are marked by the hypertrophic growth in the quantity of material and a symmetrical narrowing of fields of inquiry.

There is a difference, however. Whereas, in the hard sciences, new literature renders previous literature obsolete and thus keeps the quantity of must-reads within plausible thresholds, this is not the case with research in the humanities – and certainly not in historical research, to which religious history belongs. On the contrary, the inflation of bullet-point writing, made up of catchy titles designed for online use, shows that outdated or completely forgotten works have often retained more fertile ideas than many panels or open access pieces.[29] Contemporaneously, hyperminute overproduction and unlimited accumulation have made once-

---

27 See Paula Hamilton and James B. Gardner, eds., *The Past and Future of Public History: Developments and Challenges* (Oxford: Oxford University Press, 2017). The issue, with a focus on the religious dimension, is discussed in Marko Demantowsky, "What is Public History," in *Public History and School: International Perspectives*, ed. Marko Demantowsky (Boston-Berlin: De Gruyter, 2018), 1–38. The approach had already been outlined within a practical theology by Andries van Aarde, "What Is 'Theology' in 'Public Theology' and What Is 'Public' about 'Public Theology'?," *HTS Teologiese Studies/Theological Studies* 64 (2008). The field also has a specialized journal now, *International Journal of Public Theology*, edited by Rudolf von Sinner. An overview can be found in "Mapping Public Theologies: A Critical Analysis," in Raj Bharat Patta, *Subaltern Public Theology: Dalits and the Indian Public Sphere* (New York: Palgrave Macmillan, 2023).

28 This is the kind of territorial advocacy put in place by Vladimir Putin who, in order to justify aggression against a sovereign state, rewrote a "history" of Rus' and Russia in an essay from July 12, 2021, that year of great importance for understanding the reasons for the conflict. On that, see Stéphane Courtois, "Poutine et sa réécriture orwellienne de l'Histoire," in *Le Livre noir de Vladimir Poutine*, ed. Galia Ackerman and Stéphane Courtois (Paris: Laffont, 2022), 397–428. The same can be said regarding the acts of Hamas, which after carrying out the largest deportation and slaughter of Jews since the Shoah on October 7, 2023 and getting the predictable kind of response from the Netanyahu government, have reactivated the culture of the collective guilt of the Jews in the West by replacing "deicide" with "genocide" and the crime of the "occupation" of Palestine, whose return the Muslim Brotherhood demands in anticipation of a more enduring caliphate than the Daesh.

29 For example, I recall a note in Roger Aubert's 1959 biography of Pius IX that mentions the thought of David Urquhart, *Appel d'un protestant au Pape pour le rétablissement du droit public des nations* (Paris: C. Douniol, 1869) who, in his use of natural law, intuits the alternative later focused on by Jean-Pierre Jossua, "Effets ecclésiaux d'un discours moral," *Cristianesimo nella storia* 30 (2009): 487–490.

masterable domains too large and niches to which studies are applied too small, with nothing learned except that a case was made at some point in time and space...[30]

2

Religious history, broadly speaking, has participated in all the processes that are typical of Western culture and historical knowledge (and thus its construction, function, eclipse, and parcelization), and the same applies to the historical-critical knowledge of Christianity.

If there is a *decalage* in regard to the emergence of the concept of history in a Koselleckian sense before the 18th century, the history of Scripture, doctrines, hermeneutics, institutions, and practices of Christian communities gained its own impetus because the confessional controversy following the Reformation participated in the construction of a "modern" historiographical consciousness.[31] Let me explain: no one today would claim that works by Matthias Flacius Illyricus or Caesar Baronius[32] meet critical criteria. However, even their apologetic intent was based on the certainty that erudition was capable of saying something *true* (especially about the church), and it honed a method whereby false history could be fought and had to

---

30 See the epic essay half a century ago that set the standard in Italy, Giovanni Miccoli, "La storia religiosa," in *Storia d'Italia, vol. II, Dalla caduta dell'Impero romano al secolo XVIII*, ed. Ruggiero Romano and Corrado Vivanti (Turin: Einaudi, 1974), 429–1079: "One must strive to see particular problems within the broader context, because only in that broader context do they become problems of history, the object of the analysis and examination of a scholar of history, and not remain theology, apologetics, counter-scholasticism, or edifying moral reflection. To abstract from this is arbitrary and falsifying."

31 For example, Kaspar von Greyerz, Manfred Jakubowski-Tiessen, Thomas Kaufmann, and Hartmut Lehmann, eds., *Interkonfessionalität – Transkonfessionalität – binnenkonfessionelle Pluralität: Neue Forschungen zur Konfessionalisierungsthese*, Schriften des Vereins für Reformationsgeschichte, 201 (Gütersloh: Gütersloher Verlag, 2003).

32 See Simon Ditchfield, "What was Sacred History? (Mostly Roman) Catholic uses of the Christian Past after Trent," in *Sacred History: Uses of the Christian Past in the Renaissance World*, ed. Katherine Van Liere, Simon Ditchfield, and Howard Louthan (Oxford: Oxford University Press, 2012), 72–97.

12 —— Alberto Melloni

be beaten by a *truer* history[33] – truer because it was fueled by broader access to more authentic sources or worked with finer and more capable philosophical tools to expunge any misleading corruptions.

This not only did not prevent, but encouraged, the use of antiquarian-erudite and then historical tools as the lever of an expectation of *reformatio*, achieved by returning to an earlier state, which was revived through study. This mentality was not unique to Christianity,[34] but in different eras of Christianity it activated the fertile and very powerful myth of the early church.[35] The force of this leverage acted in schools, movements, and scholarly circles, making those "free" places targets of a hawk-eyed repression of institutions, the structures of which were at one with the conceptions of Christendom[36] – which, not for nothing, claimed to represent a historical arc from a mythical Middle Ages to a dissipated modernity.[37]

Opposite in outcomes, the same kind of mechanism has been used to describe secularization, not as a crisis of a dogmatic construction,[38] but as the slow

---

33 See Enrico Norelli, "L'autorità della Chiesa antica nelle Centurie di Magdeburgo e negli Annales del Baronio," in *Baronio storico e la Controriforma: Atti del convegno internazionale di studi, Sora 6–10 October 1979*, ed. Romeo De Maio, Luigi Gulia, and Aldo Mazzacane (Sora: Centro di studi sorani "Vincenzo Patriarca," 1982), 253–307.

34 The essay by Mircea Eliade, "The Quest for the 'Origins' of Religion," *History of Religions* 4 (1964): 154–169, is a classic.

35 Pier Cesare Bori, *Chiesa primitiva*, 2nd ed. (Brescia: Paideia, 2006, org. 1974) remains exemplary. Within the vast literature, see for example Xavier de Montclos, *Réformer l'Église: Histoire du réformisme catholique en France de la Révolution jusqu'à nos jours* (Paris: Le Cerf, 1998). For some specific cases from the conciliar era, see also Louis B. Pascoe, "Jean Gerson: The 'Ecclesia Primitiva' and Reform," *Traditio* 30 (1974): 379–409. For the revolutionary age, see Guillaume Colot, "L'Église primitive, une solution théologique à la crise traversée par le clergé français sous la Révolution," *Siècles* 35–36 (2012), https://doi.org/10.4000/siecles.1395. For the 15th century, see the recent Il Kim, "The Reform of Space for Prayer: *Ecclesia primitiva* in Nicholas of Cusa and Leon Battista Alberti," in *Nicholas of Cusa and the Making of the Early Modern World*, ed. Simon J.G. Burton, Joshua Hollmann, and Eric M. Parker (Leiden-Boston: Brill, 2019), 74–104.

36 See, for example, the overview by Lawrence N. Crumb, *The Oxford Movement and Its Leaders: A Bibliography of Secondary and Lesser Primary Sources* (Lanham, MD: Scarecrow Press, 2009); Stewart J. Brown and Peter B. Nockles, *The Oxford Movement: Europe and the Wider World 1830–1930* (Cambridge: Cambridge University Press 2012); Dominique Avon, "Une école théologique à Fourvière?," in *Les jésuites à Lyon*, ed. Étienne Fouilloux and Bernard Hours (Lyon: ENS Éditions, 2005); Marie-Dominique Chenu, *Une école de théologie: Le Saulchoir (1937)* (Paris: Cerf, 1985); and Étienne Fouilloux, *Une Église en quête de liberté* (Paris: DDB, 1998).

37 See Giuseppe Alberigo, ed., *La chrétienté en débat: Histoire, formes, et problèmes actuels* (Paris: Cerf, 1985) and Giovanni Miccoli, *Il mito della cristianità*, ed. Daniele Menozzi (Pisa: Edizioni della Normale, 2017).

38 The idea comes from Ernst Troeltsch, on which see Alfred Dumais, "Ernst Troeltsch et la sécularisation de l'histoire," *Laval théologique et philosophique* 44 (1988): 279–292.

History and the Story of the Religious Object — **13**

emancipation of consciousness in the face of a growth of alternative values that are destined, like a sacrament, to achieve this work of restoring "autonomy."[39] That goal has replaced the virulence of controversy with the advances of a critical positivism,[40] incorporated (and resized) positivist instances,[41] and gained strength in universities (both where the law divides histories between theological faculties and faculties of humanities and philosophy and where different systems of funding or establishment create models of theoretical obligation or disobligation to a confessional vision[42]).

History, therefore, has been wielded, utilized, and honed as a "tool" within the Christian religious experience by those who use it to claim "fidelity" to an arrangement deemed normative, as well as by those who use it to seek parameters capable of renewing spiritual experience or the institutions it took place within, and also by those who fear it as a subversive, countervailing power, and no less by those who use it to describe the inescapably "secular" fate of individuals and societies emancipated from religious encumbrance. Its division into principalities pleased all the hierarchs of knowledge whose impact had been alienated and diminished by the general eclipse of historical knowledge I mentioned above.

The historical-religious cognitive results obtained through this scholarly endeavor – which do not seek the proof of predictable mechanics but keep the space of the unpredictably human open through study[43] – has never, however, been determined by extrinsic criteria nor ever been measured by a misguided *methodological* a priori.

---

39 See Harvey Cox and Jan Swyngedouw, "The Myth of the Twentieth Century: The Rise and Fall of Secularization," *Japanese Journal of Religious Studies* 27 (2000): 1–13. On eschatological aporia, see Lorenz Trein, *Beobachtungen der Säkularisierung und die Grenzen der Religion* (Tübingen: Mohr Siebeck, 2023).

40 See for example, the parable described by Scott W. Hahn and Benjamin Wiker, *Politicizing the Bible: The Roots of Historical Criticism and the Secularization of Scripture 1300–1700* (New York: Herder, 2013).

41 A recent bibliography can be found in Mary Pickering, "Positivism in European Intellectual, Political, and Religious Life," in *Cambridge History of Modern European Thought*, ed. Peter E. Gordon and Warren Breckman (Cambridge: Cambridge University Press, 2019), 151–171.

42 See Francesca Cadeddu and Alberto Melloni, eds., *Report on European Religious Illiteracy* (London: Routledge, 2019).

43 Here I am following Giuseppe Galasso's, "Storicismo, filosofia, e identità italiana," paper given at "Le due culture" Quaderni di Biogem, September 11, 2011, 54–56, and Marcel Detienne, *Comment être autochtone: Du pur Athénien au Français raciné* (Paris: Seuil, 2003).

14 —— Alberto Melloni

Religious history too, as I have said, has developed a dynamic of specializations that have made individual niches more ineloquent and more crowded,[44] overproduction more unpunished and imposing,[45] and indulgence in translations more widespread, which has coincided with a decline in skills as well as the taste for critical editions.[46] But the descent into bullet-point studies, often discussed in crude and inelegant *Globish*,[47] could only produce a fixed range of criticalities comparable to those of other academic tribes.

There is a more serious and specific consequence: because the interplay between qualitative reduction and the demand for history as a "societal challenge" has made what I call the "power of synthesis" – that is, the elaboration of conceptual constructions that form and inform public opinion – disputable. No longer presided over by scholars and now used by popularizers for short-term purposes, the power of synthesis (as power) has migrated to other agents, who have inscribed it in the goals of the profession and craft. While in generalist historiography, synthesis (once exemplified by the "manual"[48]) became a cultivated journalism or multimedia popularization, in religious history it was allowed by structures and authorities that could have repressed or disciplined historical research, but never produced it.[49]

---

44 I reported a now remote phase of those lacunae in the introduction to Alberto Melloni, ed., *Dizionario del sapere storico religioso del 900*, 2 vols. (Bologna: Il Mulino, 2010), ix–xix.

45 For example, Samwah Tawil and Nada Khaddage-Soboh, "Arts, Humanities, and Social Sciences: A Scoping Review of Uncited Research," *SAGE Open* (April–June 2024): 1–6 and Gunnar Sivertsen, "Understanding and Evaluating Research and Scholarly Publishing in the Social Sciences and Humanities (SSH)," *Data and Information Management* 3/2 (2019): 61–71.

46 The praise of many authors for the aforementioned Sanders's concern about the necessity of reading sources "in the original" has been the premise for increasingly serious degenerations, the outcome of which can be seen, for example, in Edward Skibiński, "Problems with Editing and Translating Historical Sources: Some Polish Examples," *Fasciculi Archaeologiae Historicae* 28 (2014): 11–15.

47 On the problem of production quality, see Craig Hamilton, "The International State of English in Scientific Writing," *CEA [College English Association] Critic* 76 (2014): 286–292 and, more in general, on the use of an impoverished English, Elizabeth Peterson, *Making Sense of "Bad English": An Introduction to Language Attitudes and Ideologies* (Abingdon: Routledge, 2019).

48 Angela N.H. Creager, Mathias Grote, and Elaine Leong, "Learning by the Book: Manuals and Handbooks in the History of Science," *BJHS Themes* 5 (2020): 1–13.

49 In the sphere of Roman Catholicism, for example, it is interesting to note that Benedict XVI – who, as a professor, had never written a book, but only collections of essays – tried his hand at a trilogy, devoted in part to academic controversies of the 1960's, noted sharply by Pierre Gibert, "Critique, méthodologie et histoire dans l'approche de Jésus (sur: Joseph Ratzinger/Benoît XVI, Jésus de Nazareth, 1: Du baptême dans le Jourdain à la Transfiguration)," *Recherches de Science Religieuse* 96 (2008): 219–240 and Pierre Gibert, "La clarté d'une fin: L'interprétation historico-critique

At the same time, however, scholarly (hyper)production has widened the gap between research and audience in Western and Westernized cultures: one has been entrusted to peer review and the other to the market. This has created the conditions for epic short circuits, such as the one that brought an essay about a papyrus that allegedly conveyed a phrase about "Jesus's wife" to the pages of the *Harvard Theological Review* in 2014. It was a scoop that turned out to be a forgery, unrecognized as such because it was subjected to a sequence of evaluations, each of which gave their approval in a probabilistic way, instead of considering the need for an overarching knowing that weighed the set of individual verifications.[50] It would have sufficed to start from the consideration that history does not provide bulletpoint answers to bullet-point questions (mere amateurism), but rather a knowledge of the real, to realize that the papyrus did not contain evidence of an excised tradition but a deception from which historical work could and should have immunized those who practiced it and those who benefited from it.[51]

It goes without saying that this is not a new problem. Aphorism 71 of Theodor Adorno's *Minima Moralia* (written in the 1940s and published in 1951) had already summarized the famous paradox of the *pseudomenos* concerning the documentary gaps about the end met by the Führer:

> The conversion of all questions of truth into questions of power, a process that truth itself cannot escape if it is not to be annihilated by power, not only suppresses truth as in earlier

---

de la bible (sur Joseph Ratzinger/Benoît XVI, Jésus de Nazareth, 2: De l'entrée à Jérusalem à la Résurrection)," *Recherches de Science Religieuse* 99 (2011): 511–527. Less severe is Pierre Lassave, "Joseph Ratzinger-Benoît XVI, Jésus de Nazareth, Deuxième partie, De l'entrée à Jérusalem à la Résurrection," *Archives de sciences sociales des religions* 156 (2011): 262–263.

50 Karen L. King, "Jesus said to them, 'My wife...': A New Coptic Papyrus Fragment," *Harvard Theological Review* 107 (2014): 131–159. The epic fail was due to the fact that, discarding the objections made in the same issue by an Egyptologist such as Leo Depuydt, the author became convinced that she had found a reference that did not stand up to the painstaking verification carried out by *The Atlantic Monthly*; that instead of evaluating the individual scientific verifications (papyrus, ink, etc.) separately, she discovered that it was not a discovery, but a summation of negligence, perhaps due to laziness, sloppiness, and above all, deference to a post-truthful logic according to which in any case a papyrus (even if it was sold by a Deutsche Demokratische Republik museum official) could say something of value because everyone was silent about it. See Ariel Sabar, *Veritas: A Harvard Professor, a Con Man, and the Gospel of Jesus's Wife* (New York: Doubleday, 2020).

51 This was the point of a famous essay by Hayden White, "The Politics of Historical Interpretation: Discipline and De-Sublimation," *Critical Inquiry* 9 (1982): 113–137 and its vigorous rebuttal by Wulf Kansteiner, "Hayden White's Critique of the Writing of History," *History and Theory* 32 (1982): 273–295. The burning nature of the issue emerged, for example, in an essay by Emma Green, "The Right Side of History: How Should Historians Respond to the Urgency of this Current Political Moment?," *The New Yorker*, March 7, 2023.

despotic orders, but has attacked the very heart of the distinction between true and false, which the hirelings of logic were in any case diligently working to abolish. So Hitler, of whom no one can say whether he died or escaped, survives.[52]

The question of truth that Adorno poses is the one that ultimately decides, provisionally and at the same time inescapably, the inherent "provisional" or "unnatural" value of historical inquiry.[53]

3

The question I ask myself and to which I propose answering in the positive is thus whether historical-religious knowledge can know and recognize the normative structure that defines and validates its knowledge, without starting from a philosophy of history, but only from its object.

Scholarly tradition says that this has been the ambition and goal of research that is aware of the broad contexts proper to it,[54] that is responsive to attempts to reconcile cause-and-effect connections at full speed and is capable of tasking itself with the production of limited and provisional truths.

Part of this tradition and the normative structure that defines it is the conviction that sources are never "evidence" of a tribunalization,[55] but images reflected by the pieces of the shattered mirror of an actual present, pieces that have come to us on a path decided by power and/or chance and that are handed over to us to be evaluated as a whole, knowing that the source has not been designed to copy-paste into notes but to tell or to lie, or both. Indeed, the source is an artifact that conveys a dilemma that is constant and constantly revisited by study that can only be

---

52 Theodor Adorno, *Minima Moralia: Reflections on a Damaged Life*, trans. Edmund F.N. Jephcott (London-New York: Verso, 1974), 109. I have a well-founded fear that Adorno also counted, as among the mercenaries of logic, Odo Marquard and his polemic on the tribunalization of history that he imputed to the Frankfurt School. On his thought, see Brian O'Connor, "Adorno: Philosophy of History," in *Adorno: Key Concepts*, ed. Deborah Cook (London: Routledge, 2008), 179–195.

53 I owe the expression about history as "provisional" knowledge to Denis Pelletier. See also the lecture by Sam Wineburg, "Why Historical Thinking is Not about History," *History News* (2016): 13–16, which echoes his theses already expressed in Sam Wineburg, *Historical Thinking and Other Unnatural Acts* (Philadelphia: Temple University Press, 2001).

54 He explains this in the foreword to one of his essays, as cited in note 30 above, Giovanni Miccoli, "La storia religiosa."

55 Marquard and Melloni, *La storia che giudica*, and Odo Marquard, *Zukunft braucht Herkunft: Philosophische Essays* (Stuttgart: Reclam, 2003).

latitudinal, sympathetic, and patient (as would be given in a catalog of ancient virtues) or, to put it in more "up to date" terms, emancipated in the face of archival fetishes, exacting in the face of the sly laziness of pdfs.

In the case of religious history, these attitudes must take into account the fact that those who produced the source (the individual, community, or proceeding) have, by definition, measured themselves against a normative given, to which they believed or would have liked to believe themselves faithful, not always aspiring to set out on the path that (pseudo-)historical teleologies have prepared for them, making everything a deniable political or ideological clue.[56] From this point of view then, the historical-religious specifically contributes to denying intellectual legitimacy to the explicit or disguised pursuit of those "inexorable laws of historical destiny" that Karl Popper, in 1944, defined as the miserable condition of the "partial science" that he called "historicism."[57]

Popper's was an early requiem for a historiographical mechanism that, according to the philosopher, served in his day to deceive the masses hypnotized by fascist and Stalinist totalitarian ideologies. But, in its own way, it is still today a call to continue reaching out toward that fragment of truth that, in the case of historical-religious research, is *a* truth that takes into account that there is another truth in the object, a truth by which it is to be understood and judged and that can never be set aside as something "doctrinaire" to be purged as if it were debris.

---

56 At this point it seems obvious to me but, to give a nod to Milbank's caveat: "Once, there was no 'secular.' And the secular was not latent, waiting to fill more space with the steam of the 'purely human,' when the pressure of the sacred was relaxed. Instead there was the single community of Christendom, with its dual aspects of *sacerdotium* and *regnum*. The *saeculum*, in the medieval era, was not a space, a domain, but a time the interval between fall and eschaton where coercive justice, private property, and impaired natural reason must make shift to cope with the unredeemed effects of sinful humanity," John Milbank, *Theology and Social Theory: Beyond Secular Reason* (Oxford: Blackwell, 1990), 9.

57 I think it can be said, however, that the historical positivist mechanism that Popper polemicized with is now eclipsed like the Marxist dogmatics on which he depended: the historiography that holds that neither sources nor fact are proof or evidence of anything makes it perfectly easy to share Popper's conclusion that "it is not possible for us to observe or to describe a whole piece of the world, or a whole piece of nature; in fact, not even the smallest whole piece may be so described, since all description is necessarily selective," see Karl Popper, "The Poverty of Historicism," *Economica* 11/42 (1942): 86–103. On his thought, see Malachi Haim Hacohen, *Karl Popper, The Formative Years, 1902–1945: Politics and Philosophy in Interwar Vienna* (Cambridge: Cambridge University Press, 2000).

18 —— Alberto Melloni

4

While there is a history (or a historicism) that gives historical-religious knowledge its specific object, the question remains whether it is necessary to name it, what name it should be given, and whether it should establish a common semantics. In fact, naming that production of knowledge has fueled an interminable debate made up of options whose antagonism has distracted from the essential point, namely, that what decides the quality of knowledge is not the term used to categorize it, but what connotes it.

As is well known, those defending the label of "religious studies"[58] have shifted from the idea that there is a separate and identified approach. The French formulation (which has been borrowed in part in Italy) of *sciences religieuses* has cleared a space declared immune from any theological or political conditioning.[59] The Italian phrasing (from a title of Ernesto Buonaiuti) of *storia religiosa*[60] was defined in contrast to a "history of religions," which considered a comparative dexterity its hallmark. In German, *Religionwissenschaft* declared a complete otherness with respect to denominational histories and histories of and to doctrines, erecting an intransigent barrier around an impermeable category.[61]

For those who still owe some debt to Saul Kripke's reading,[62] this dispute takes place in a room where the strong smell of elephant still lingers, and the elephant's

---

58 The debate half a century ago began with Schubert M. Ogden, "Theology and Religious Studies: Their Difference and the Difference It Makes," *Journal of the American Academy of Religion* 46 (1978): 3–17. Understandably, the radical position of Timothy Fitzgerald, *The Ideology of Religious Studies* (Oxford-New York: Oxford University Press, 2000) has been criticized.

59 The argument in Pierre Gisel, "Les sciences religieuses: Données et défis; État des lieux: Des richesses et des décentrements, mais pour quoi?, " *Revue des sciences religieuses* 95 (2021): 71–90 is flawless.

60 *Storia religiosa cristiana* (Christian Religious History) was the title of the course Ernesto Buonaiuti was permitted to teach after the university that he had been expelled from for not swearing allegiance to fascism was liberated. Useful only for its bibliography is Francesco Mores, "Historiae ecclesiasticae disputationes: Ernesto Buonaiuti tra metodologia e finzione," in Ernesto Buonaiuti, *Lezioni di storia ecclesiastica: L'antichità, Storia e Letteratura* (Rome: Edizioni di Storia e Letteratura, 2016), vii–xxxv.

61 See Klaus Hock, *Einführung in die Religionswissenschaft* (Darmstadt: Wissenschaftliche Buchgesellschaft, 2002).

62 Saul Kripke, *Naming and Necessity* (Oxford: Basil Blackwell, 1980). Studies on the work can be found in Igal Kuart, "Kripke's Belief Puzzle," in *Studies in the Philosophy of Mind*, ed. Peter A. French, Theodore E. Uehling, and Howard K. Wettstein (Minneapolis: University of Minnesota

name is theology. It is an elephant capable of eliciting phobic reactions, such as that of the aforementioned bull of excommunication against a forum such as the European Academy of Religion.[63] It was a grotesque but revelatory episode because it envisioned the forum producing historical-critical knowledge of religious fact as a tribe that has to defend itself against knowledge that would contaminate the *reine Rasse* of true researchers and their "academic" study of an object that has been consigned not from history but from a decontamination center.

Concretely put, it goes without saying that there is an ideological use of theology that flattens investigation of foreign criteria and is, for that very reason, inadmissible (as happens to be the similarly ideological use of law, sociology, philosophy, economics, and even biology). It is, by the way, inadmissible for an internal reason, because the ideological use of theology is not theology but a form of religious propaganda. It attempts or wants to make use of rationality for purposes of power. It detests historical-critical knowledge because it fears making an already quivering faith tremble, and it only relaxes before that cloyingly providentialist apologetics of a God of the gaps that is supposed to provide the keys to interpreting an otherwise indecipherable history.

Historical research should have nothing but pity and scorn for this homespun theology. It would be a concrete harm to historical-religious knowledge if that pseudo-science were conceded a banner of knowledge that belongs to others such as – and I am mentioning, almost at random, some from recent centuries – that into which Friedrich Hegel poured his Christology,[64] to which Martin Heidegger gave his Pauline commentaries,[65] where Bernard Lonergan elaborated the category of self-

---

Press, 1986), 287–325; Jonathan Berg, *Naming, Necessity, and More: Explorations in the Philosophical Work of Saul Kripke* (New York: Palgrave Macmillan, 2014); and Andrea Bianchi, "Back to the Golden Age: Saul Kripke's Naming and Necessity and Twenty-First Century Philosophy," *Theoria* 88 (2022): 278–295.

63 It was found guilty of including *all* scientific disciplines "that traverse – or are traversed by – religious experience," and thus barring neither theology as a producer of materials that historical-religious research takes as its object of study nor theology as a science in its own right that disputes and dialogues within its own epistemological framework.

64 Emilio Brito, *La christologie de Hegel, Verbum Crucis* (Paris: Beauchesne, 1983). His work on German philosophers continued with the no less interesting Emilio Brito, *La pneumatologie de Schleiermacher* (Leuven: Peeters, 1994) and Emilio Brito, *La theologie de Fichte* (Paris: Cerf, 2007).

65 See Mario Fischer, *Religiöse Erfahrung in der Phänomenologie des frühen Heidegger* (Göttingen: Vandenhoeck & Ruprecht, 2013) and, more recently, Isabella Guanzini, "The Pauline Understanding of Life in the Young Heidegger (1920–21)," *Interdisciplinary Journal for Religion and Transformation in Contemporary Society* 5 (2019): 120–135.

appropriation,[66] or where Wolfhart Pannenberg established history as the locus of revelation.[67] It is the knowledge of those who have made extensive use of historical research in their theologizing that has illuminated areas previously inaccessible to historical inquiry.[68]

A theology worthy of the name challenges its results with the criteria and keys proper to its investigations. In this debate, it earns that title not only when it offers itself as a producer of sources (that is, as the object of a history of theology[69]) but also when it offers keys to historical knowledge that actually work or have worked, have inspired choices or debunked acts, and that – on par with those that that knowledge draws from, such as economics, geography, and art – serve to define the object more precisely.

5

The object to which religious history is applied decides its epistemic status and demands recourse to any tool that can provide a knowledge free from ostracism, extrinsicism, and hierarchical constraints in order to tap into the limited amount available to rational exploration.

History, thus, is the history of experience and the conceptions that nurture it, if one were to put it in a formula. It is the history of beliefs and practices that are the outcome of long-lasting processes, defined by change and differentiation to other experiences and other conceptions, conditioned by linguistic paradigms, institutional dynamics, material and immaterial cultures, and varied lived experiences.

Everything is and is only history – the history of religious experience does not need to swap clothes with other forms of knowledge. It knows that it cannot ignore doctrines, hermeneutics, institutions, ethics, rights, theologies, forms of worship,

---

66 See, for example, the essays in James L. Marsh, ed., *Lonergan in the World: Self-Appropriation, Otherness, and Justice* (Toronto: Toronto University Press, 2014).

67 See, also, for example, the essays collected in Gunther Wenz, ed., *Vom wahrhaft Unendlichen: Metaphysik und Theologie bei Wolfhart Pannenberg* (Göttingen: Vandenhoeck & Ruprecht, 2016).

68 It is an endless litany in which, after Möhler and Harnack, many other names can be listed, among whom I would like to mention at least Marie-Dominique Chenu, Yves Congar, Henri De Lubac, David Tracy, Aloys Grillmeyer, Peter Hünhermann, Georg Kretschmar, John Meyendorff, Giuseppe Ruggieri, Rudolf Schnackenburg, etc.

69 By way of example see the success of Alister E. McGrath, *Historical Theology: An Introduction to the History of Christian Thought*, 3rd. ed. (Hoboken, NJ: Wilely Blackwell, 2023).

convictions, or faiths that a jargon that claims to be objectifying declares to have descended from "beliefs" (often leaving the implication that much patience is needed toward those who are credulous in the face of beliefs[70]).

History is unyielding in denying the bigoted conceit that calls "faith" a miserable ersatz of tenuous certainties – waved as indispensable fetishes for understanding a sacred text or an event or a community. History is uncompromising in denying the secular bigotry that fails to understand that those who study people, groups, and institutions – within which act inner persuasions of an intellectual and even mystical kind – are confronted with a driving force that is even more real than the "political motivations" invoked in the face of what one would not want to attribute to the prudish and profound intentionality that is forbidden to the historian in its origins that are immersed in consciousness, but not in its outcomes, which surface in reality.[71]

6

The knowability of the object of historical-religious study, therefore, involves experiences and conceptions, needs premises and criteria, but ultimately achieves results: which are not all included in the premises or automatically produced by the criteria adopted.

This is demonstrated (and in this case I would truly use the term "demonstrated") by the dispute between Hubert Jedin and Giuseppe Alberigo on the object of church history half a century ago. Jedin had written that church history receives its *object* from theology, meaning that, for a historian of the Catholic Church, it was the way in which the Catholic Church represented itself that constituted its methodological perimeter. On the contrary, Alberigo argued that it was history itself that conveyed the *object* – church as a knowable object, which he later developed into his thesis

---

70 See Tim Crane, *The Meaning of Belief* (Cambridge, MA: Harvard University Press, 2017).

71 Unless we resort to the anti-realism of Michael Dummet, *Truth and the Past* (New York: Columbia University Press, 2004), according to which the extent of the set of truths will correspond to that of knowable propositions. On the convergences between Dummet's anti-realism and Putnam's internal realism, see Hilary Putnam, *The Collapse of the Fact/Value Dichotomy and Other Essays* (Cambridge, MA: Harvard University Press, 2002); and Karin M. Johannesson, "Non-Metaphysical Realism: A Dummett-Inspired Implementation of Putnam's Internal Realism," *European Journal for Philosophy of Religion* 6 (2014): 3–18.

on the connaturality between Christianity and its history.[72] Personally, I identify with Alberigo's position, having had the privilege of being his pupil. That said, there is an objective observation to be made concerning the cognitive quality of Alberigo's and Jedin's histories of the Council of Trent and the Second Vatican Council. The offspring of two incompatible methodological options, they are both unavoidable, even today, for those who wish to understand Roman Catholicism in this half-millennium, because the cognitive result they achieve is the same.

The hypothesis I would like to conclude with, then, is that it is the manner and tact of recognizing the primacy of one's object (I say this in view of Neil Tennant's "wondering whether"[73]) that determines, downstream of every working hypothesis and every theoretical postulate, a producer of knowledge. It sees the object – not a procedure, method, algorithm, or set of "laws," but "that *quid* that we call historical meaning."[74]

7

The primacy of the object, to conclude, is effective if it commands a heuristic question: a question that, as such (but also in its Koselleckian Vorgriff) traverses the history of historiography and, in the age of the dematerialization of source media (quod vulgo dicitur "digital humanities"), traverses the question of the spatial-temporal extension of the Christian fact.

Nineteenth century Germanic-minded historiography had taken the measure of this problem and created "ancillary" disciplines (archaeological, epigraphical, numismatic, papyrological, codicological, etc.) necessary for refining a set of knowledge and tools (that today we would call formats or platforms, that is, repertories, registers, *momumenta, corpora*, huge collections of knowledge) in which great historians tried their hand at becoming the first users of tools produced to

---

72 Giuseppe Alberigo, "Cristianesimo come storia e teologia confessante," foreword to Marie-Dominique Chenu, *Le Saulchoir: Una scuola di teologia*, trans. N.F. Reviglio (Casale Monferrato: Marietti, 1982).

73 Neil Tennant, *The Taming of the True* (Oxford-New York: Oxford University Press, 1997). Against, for example, see Florian Steinberger, "Tennant on Multiple Conclusions," *Logique et Analyse* 51/201 (2008): 49–55.

74 Such as Cantimori wrote in the foreword to Giuseppe Alberigo, *I vescovi italiani al concilio di Trento* (Florence: Vallecchi, 1959), viii.

excavate unexplored terrain. The queen of the handmaids, however, was source discovery, source reading, and source analysis.

Without ceding to a nostalgia for "the heuristics of the ancients," it must be acknowledged that, today, there is no Mommsen of new access to sources.[75] Rather, looking at the production, one has the well-founded suspicion that a computer-assisted cherry picking has restricted the study of and access to sources to a series of arbitrary acts called "core sampling," which is conditioned by what is accessible via the internet and that gives space to those who line up the little they know from rummaging through the great digital emporium of the latter, abusively calling their ignorance "cultural" history. It is what I think could be called a mannerist historiography,[76] shameful in itself and damaging for all because it infests the town square of knowledge (which is also a marketplace) with counterfeit currency. Mannerist historiography might seem acceptable to an extrinsic checklist. It finds a few sources, retrieves a bit of bibliography, demarcates a geographic and temporal zone, sprinkles its prose with catchphrases of the trade,[77] and produces nothing that would make that *extra* crumb of truth known, which is the craft of a historian. While libraries are full of great works of synthesis, capable of spanning centuries and geographies by fixing essential paradigms in the reader's mind and arousing unexplored questions, the "tourism" use of history runs rampant, destroying critical ground and preparing for a culture where every subject has its "Handbook," "Companion," or its "Atlas."

On the other hand, there is a nascent "heuristic of the moderns," where AI could serve a purpose: not only to put out of commission the mannerism of those who read without quoting, those who quote without reading, and those who read only to copy; and not just to break the spell generated by the so-called "digital

---

75 See Jörg Rogge, ed., *Cultural History in Europe: Institutions, Themes, Perspectives* (Bielefeld: transcript, 2011); Philippe Poirrier, ed., *L'histoire culturelle: Un "tournant mondial" dans l'historiographie?* (Dijon: Universitaires de Dijon, 2008); and an interesting detour in Denis Pelletier and Florian Michel, eds., *Pour une histoire sociale et culturelle de la théologie: Autour de Claude Langlois* (Turnhoudt: Brepols, 2023).

76 I dedicated an essay to a piece by Matteo Al Kalak (built on the same structure adopted in his later *Fuoco e fiamme: Storia e geografia dell'inferno*, Turin: Einaudi, 2024): Alberto Melloni, "Sur le maniérisme historiographique: Notes à l'occasion d'une 'histoire de l'eucharistie'," *Revue d'histoire ecclésiastique* 117 (2024): 267–276.

77 For example, "I rely on the studies of...," "this is not the place where...," "limited to the scope drawn by...." I recall the antiquated but delightful essay by Jack H. Hexter, "The Rhetoric of History," *History & Theory* 6 (1967): 3–13.

humanities,"[78] which forget that "digital" is only an ink that does not stain but also does not produce any of what historical and historical-religious knowledge needs within it *ex nihilo*.

Artificial Intelligence for Humanities could make a contribution here. AI, actually, is neither artificial nor intelligent. It is a human system of constructing correlations within quantities of data and a quantity of correlations that cannot be constrained by the temporal limits of human existence.[79] It is how these systems of correlation can act in understanding the patrimonial degree of sources of historical-religious knowledge, the diachronic and global extension of which allows for a *mole* similar to Avogadro's constant.[80]

The primacy of the object, then, restores legitimacy to those intentions whose origin, locked in the inviolable temple of consciousness, a historian cannot explore,

---

78 On the final frontiers, see, for example, Zhiqing Zhang, Wanyi Song, and Peng Liu, "Making and Interpreting: Digital Humanities as Embodied Action," *Humanities and Social Sciences Communications* 11/13 (2024). It is a fact that mountains of digital works circulating today, authorized or not, are not only characterized by errors, but have also not generated great tools (Potthast) or great collections (ACO) or enabled an equipment of the great archives. The reason for this is perfectly understandable: if we compare them to the technological leaps that made Jean Bolland's work possible – the work of Giovanni Domenico Mansi and Jacques Paul Migne, H. Welter's anastatic texts – we can see with the naked eye that the digital humanities have affected time but not the quantity of knowledge, which requires the construction and reconstruction of connections.

79 The logic of "digital twins," for example, builds models of cities or organisms on which to test the effect of policy or therapeutic decisions so as to assess the outcome of variations and reactions in the face of politics or therapies. What is interesting from a cognitive point of view (what makes the digital twin "work") is not the knowledge of the particular points, but the study of their correlations – which, in history, constitutes the proper dimension of that which exceeds the subject's perception.

80 Because, as I mentioned, the primacy of the object of historical-religious knowledge demands a revisiting of its global, as well as diachronic, nature. This can and must take place first of all at the level of becoming aware of the depth of one's own responses, which arise not only from a Eurocentrism that is deep-seated and instilled throughout the sphere of influence of Western domination. We cannot, for example, tell of the missionary world without balancing the reverse momentum of individuals and economic fluctuations. But then we have to contend with the Quebecois paralogism – that one implemented by a prolific Canadian theologian who always finds in Quebec history the evidence of the great processes of pre-conciliar, conciliar, and post-conciliar Catholicism. He finds them not because he creates or falsifies them: he finds them because they are obvious and because they are simply the refraction of general processes and therefore a pure phenomenon that certainly deserves to be studied and comprehended without inferring a paradigmatic quality that it cannot have. They correspond to the effort one would make to prove (following Bertold Brecht's famous *Fragen eines lesenden Arbeiters*) that Caesar defeated the Gauls and that he had "at least one cook with him" ("wenigstens einen Koch bei sich").

the effects of which, however, can be found in lives and mindsets, incubators of thoughts and gestures.

The subject's consciousness, in fact, contains a bundle of intentions that can be simplified by reducing them to an age-old essence.[81] Certainly, they can easily be transformed into evidence for a theological position. Or they can be grasped by recovering the full extent of Droysen's paradigm: history is such – and religious history is such – if it is *independent* of theology and law (and, today, one might add independent of sociology, anthropology, economics, AI, etc.). But it is independent not if/because it ignores them, but because/if it knows how to make use of them.

8

In the flux of paradigms that come and go in the history of every area of study, historical-religious studies have one that accompanies it. It is that it sees in each of the disciplines that engage it, not bodies to be expelled, but the whetstone that – used with the proper caveats – serves to sharpen conclusions that draw on a small, specific, integrable portion of truth, but one that it aspires to.[82]

---

81 One could dwell on the militant Irish prisoner in Ulster, Bobby Sands, dying on a hunger strike. It was waged from a Catholic nationalist sentiment that was undoubtedly political, but not only. The battle for a political-confessional unification of Ireland was inspired by nationalist sentiment, but included yet another reincarnation of the myth of Christendom, to which – it goes without saying – Pope John Paul II offered his support, see Margaret M. Scull, "The Catholic Church and the Hunger Strikes of Terence MacSwiney and Bobby Sands," *Irish Political Studies* 31 (2015): 282–299.
82 Myers and Kaye, eds., *The Faith of Fallen Jews.*

Alexander Kulik
Naming God and Other Challenges of Transcultural Monotheism[1]

Abstract: The pivotal shift in the evolution of Abrahamic religions occurred when the Hebrew faith was transplanted onto Greek soil, giving rise to what may be termed "transcultural monotheism." This linguo-theological transformation aligned with other important shifts—not only political developments that led to internationalization of the Greek language but also more profound cultural processes that replaced myth with speculative thought. In other words, Moses' spiritual message had to await Alexander's political infrastructure and Athenian intellectual tools to enable Judeo-Greek creativity. Intended to meet the inner needs of the Hellenistic Jewish community, it eventually became a factor of universal impact.

This expansion of Second Temple Judaism, including its Christian variation, beyond the Semitic realm presented new challenges. Unique theological constructs anchored in specific linguistic forms and structures faced the necessity of adaptation. This was particularly evident with respect to the core concept of Jewish thought—the one and only "God," the sole creator and ruler of the universe. It proved no easy task to pick a name for such a referent that essentially lies beyond any taxonomy—i.e., unknowable and, therefore, unnamable.

The introduction of Greek terms for this concept, as well as their equivalents in other languages, proceeded not without deliberation or resistance. The inherent inadequacy of any term for the concept of the monotheistic God led and continues to lead to unceasing attempts to explore alternative terminology.

This paper aims to reconstruct previously overlooked considerations behind a Judeo-Greek innovation in religious terminology, with a focus on its key element—Hellenization of the Hebrew name of God. The suggested reconstruction may affect

---

1 I want to begin my lecture with words of appreciation for those of my colleagues who have shown unequivocal and unreserved support for my country in its struggle against the forces of evil that promote hatred, deception, and violence not only in the land of Israel but in every place they can reach: וַאֲבָרְכָה מְבָרְכֶיךָ וּמְקַלֶּלְךָ אָאֹר. We mourn all the innocent lives lost, especially of the innocent children who wore uniforms to defend their homes and a world that aspires to remain free, safe and prosperous, and we pray for peace and justice for all: לְקְרֹא שְׁנַת רָצוֹן לַה׳ וְיוֹם נָקָם לֵא-לֹהֵינוּ לְנַחֵם כָּל אֲבֵלִים.

This lecture briefly presents the main theses of my paper "Counting on God's Name: The Numerology of Nomina Sacra" (Harvard Theological Review, 2025).

Open Access. © 2025 the author(s), published by De Gruyter. This work is licensed under the Creative Commons Attribution 4.0 International License.
https://doi.org/10.1515/9783112218907-003

our perspective on several fields of knowledge and shed light on some unresolved questions, including the problems of biblical isopsephism, early Jewish and Christian numeric symbolism, the history of *nomina sacra* (including the question of their Jewish vs. Christian origins), and early binitarian theology.

The case I am going to present today lies at the intersection of linguistic and theological developments, both of which have played a crucial role in shaping the religious landscape of the last two millennia. Introducing the concepts of "Judeo-Greek linguo-theological revolution" and "transcultural monotheism" and focusing on their connection, seeing the former as the catalyst of the latter and the latter as an unplanned result of the former, may help us understand many phenomena of religious thought that we today take for granted but which originated in Hellenistic Judaism.

The most pivotal shift in the evolution of Abrahamic religions occurred when Hebrew faith was transplanted onto Greek soil, giving rise to what may be termed "transcultural monotheism." This linguo-theological transformation aligned with important shifts, not only political developments leading to the internationalization of the Greek language but also more profound cultural processes amending, augmenting, and replacing myth with speculative thought. In other words, Moses' spiritual message had to await Alexander's political infrastructure and Athenian intellectual tools to enable Judeo-Greek creativity. The transcultural expansion of Second Temple Judaism, including its Christian variant, beyond the Semitic realm brought new challenges. Jewish original theological constructs, bound to their idiosyncratic linguistic forms and built into specific paradigmatic structures, had to change. The new linguistic tools intended to meet the inner needs of the Hellenistic Jewish community eventually became a factor of universal impact.

Although early Judaism and Christianity were not the only ancient religions with universal ambitions, their universalization became the most consequential and is incomparably better documented. Changing historical conditions of the "old" and "new" Israel brought them into collision with ancient "global languages." We see Aramaic and Phoenician languages removed from this status by Greek-speaking Macedonians and Latin-speaking Romans after the Alexandrian and Punic wars; the rise of the Latin West and Latin diglossia versus new ecclesiastical languages of the Eastern churches; Islam's successful solution to this tension – by imposing the language of religion as an everyday language on part of the former Roman imperial territory; the Reformation which challenged linguistic hierarchy and introduced ethnic, so-called "national" languages. This meeting is conducted in English, and who knows what awaits us in the future. Another manifestly universal language is numbers, and we shall see today that its potential as such could be perceived already in late antiquity.

Thus, we enter here a field of "Language and Religion," seen usually through the lens of translation studies, a field shared by post-structuralism, analytical philosophy, and cognitive sciences. I will mention here only the tension between Willard Quine's thesis of the "Indeterminacy of Translation"[2] and Donald Davidson's theory of "Radical Interpretation."[3] The former states that conceptual systems are too holistic for to be adequately translated (which for our purposes means the impossibility of what we call transcultural religion), while the latter postulates that conceptual systems can be related.

We can discern both approaches already in antiquity, where we find a conflict between the innate conflicting tendencies of linguistic particularism and transcultural ambition. Linguistic particularism understood that a change of language is a change of god. If names of God in the same language are his hypostases, then all the more so in different languages. Religion is a system of concepts that crumbles in translation. On the other hand, the practical needs of an increasingly integrating humanity left no choice but to integrate conceptual systems, although the question of the extent to which these integrative efforts proved adequate may remain an open one even now.

Greek-speaking Jews (not only of Alexandria and Antioch but also of Jerusalem, Caesarea and Tiberias) had to deal with this challenge, and they developed solutions that paved the way for transcultural monotheisms. For this purpose, instead of undertaking the impossible task of, in Julia Kristeva's terms, "transposition of one sign scheme into another," they gradually developed a new conceptual system based on both Hebrew and Greek systems.

With this understanding in mind, I started a series of studies of early Jewish (including under this term also early Christian) religious terminology whose original meanings and functions can be elucidated only by the complex and reciprocal relations of Hebrew and Greek. I found a certain encouragement and corroboration of the validity of this approach in the fact that its mere application enabled "desk discoveries," that is, recognition of phenomena "hidden in plain view." The first two studies deal with the terms for "Lord" and his cardinal mode of manifestation – "revelation" – two terms that in Greek, I claim, make sense only in their transcultural and translinguistic existence.

---

2 Quine, W. V. *Word and Object*. Cambridge, MA: Technology Press of the MIT, 1960. P. IXff.

3 Davidson, D. "Radical Interpretation". *Dialectica* 27 (1973). P. 313–328 (Reprinted in *Inquiries into Truth and Interpretation*, 2nd ed. Oxford: Oxford University Press, 2001. P. 125–140). Cf. Frankberry, N. K. and H. H. Penner (eds.). *Language, Truth and Religious Belief*. Chicago: The Univ. of Chicago, 1999. Part IV.

Both studies have been recently accepted by the *Harvard Theological Review*. One of them has already been published and is accessible online[4]. It examines various ways in which apocalyptic studies can benefit from the introduction of the term and concept of *gilayon* (גליון), a reconstructed Hebrew counterpart of the Judeo-Greek ἀποκάλυψις "apocalypse." This original Hebrew term combined the meanings of "book/scroll" and "revelation," which combination refers to a central image of early Jewish revealed literature and could serve to define an important corpus, the boundaries of which might well overlap with what is understood by the "genre apocalypse" in modern research. This reconstructed concept uncovers additional meanings and associations, among them a bilingual word-play between *gilayon* and *evangelion* (and possibly *logion*). We find documented associations between the two in Pauline and other Greek usages as well as in the term *aven-gilayon* of rabbinic literature, which may shed light inter alia on the genre-belonging of the gospels.

Another accepted paper, dealing with the name of God, is still forthcoming, and I will briefly present its main points here.

1 Naming God

Naming is one of the fundamental devices of cognition. Since the latter is based, as noticed already by Aristotle, on our ability to recognize commonalities and differences,[5] it is not easy to pick a name for a referent which, being completely unique, at the same time also contains all other referents within itself. Such a referent remains essentially beyond any taxonomy—that is, unknowable and, therefore, unnamable. However, our ability and need to contemplate such an entity makes its naming necessary. Indeed, over the course of history such names have been achieved through diverse and often interdependent modes of revelation, tradition, and speculation.

The central idea of Jewish thought—the concept of the one and only God, the sole creator and ruler of the universe—developed through elaboration of a set of terms enabling the possibility of referring to this original theological construct.

---

4 Alexander Kulik, "*Gilayon* and 'Apocalypse': Reconsidering an Early Jewish Concept and Genre." *Harvard Theological Review* 116.2 (2023). P. 190–227 (https://www.cambridge.org/core/journals/harvard-theological-review/article/gilayon-and-apocalypse-reconsidering-an-early-jewish-concept-and-genre/DACB90C388C2CD98E768379BFED593FA).

5 See, e.g., Aristotle, *Met.* 10.1054b; 3.999a; cf. W. Quine, "Natural Kinds," in *Ontological Relativity and Other Essays* (ed. J. Kim and E. Sosa; New York: Columbia University Press, 1969) 114–138, at 116.

These Hebrew designations of God—his names, titles, and attributes, some borrowed from existing cults and others unprecedentedly original—underwent transformation as they evolved towards a monotheistic conception.[6] This transformation was as semantic as it was structural. That is, being integrated into monotheistic usage, these pre-monotheistic terms underwent an evolution of their meanings. By developing and complementing each other, they came to form a new conceptual structure (or, more precisely, multiple structures) of the only God and his characteristics.

2 Translating God's name

Devising names for God is a linguo-theological development that has, in fact, never ended. It continues in our days, having been transplanted to multiple cultural contexts. However, during certain phases of history it accelerated, becoming more productive and influential. The transformation of religious terminology that occurred when the Hebrew faith was exported onto Greek language became the basis for all subsequent developments. This Hellenization of God was similar to and different from the long, painful, and inspiring process of the reduction (or, if you prefer, promotion) of old Semitic deities to the names and titles of the Hebrew God. Both processes were intercultural and had immense consequences for religious and secular thought. The main difference is that the later process was shorter in duration, has much better documentation, and belongs to the period when speculative thought began to displace myth.

Among the nearly one hundred terms and metaphoric and descriptive epithets applied to God in the Hebrew Bible and early post-biblical Jewish literature,[7] the

---

6 Among relatively general or recent works on Hebrew divine names, see, e.g., Oskar Grether, *Name und Wort Gottes im Alten Testament* (Giessen, 1934); Lawrence H. Schiffman, "The Use of Divine Names," in his *Sectarian Law in the Dead Sea Scrolls: Courts, Testimony and the Penal Code* (BJS 33; Chico, CA: Scholars Press, 1983) 133–54; Otto Kaiser, *Der Gott des Alten Testaments* (3 vols.; Göttingen, 1993, 1998, 2003); Adelheid Ruck-Schröder, *Der Name Gottes und der Name Jesu. Eine neutestamentliche Studie* (WMANT; Neukirchen-Vluyn, 1999); Christiane Zimmermann, *Die Namen des Vaters. Studien zu ausgewählten neutestamentlichen Gottesbezeichnungen vor ihrem frühjüdischen und paganen Sprachhorizont* (Leiden: Brill, 2007) 12–17; David Porreca, "Divine Names: A Cross-Cultural Comparison (Papyri Graecae Magicae, Picatrix, Munich Handbook)," *Magic, Ritual, and Witchcraft* 5.1 (2010) 17–29.
7 See, e.g., the list of Greek terms in Ralph Marcus, "Divine Names and Attributes in Hellenistic Literature," *Proceedings of the American Academy for Jewish Research* 2 (1931–1932) 45–120. See also Zimmermann, *Die Namen des Vaters*.

most significant and least translatable was the name of four letters (the Tetragram). The most common equivalent for the Tetragram (on the meanings of which, see below) came to be Greek κύριος (often in its contracted form —κ͞ς͞), which combined a diverse set of meanings ranging from the mundane "master, lord" to the royal human or divine "Lord." This polysemy has been partly inherited through the biblical usage by the English word *Lord* and its equivalents in other languages, such as *Dominus, Signor, Herr, Господь*, et cetera. The introduction of κύριος, as well as its equivalents in many languages, proceeded not without deliberation or resistance. The inadequacy of any term to be applied to the concept of the monotheistic God caused and continues to cause unceasing attempts to introduce alternative terminology. These philosophical and taxonomic difficulties were compounded by cultic and magical considerations, as well as by the social-religious concerns of group identity.

The demand for alternatives and surrogates appeared already in Hebrew usage. In parallel with the development of the Greek tradition that was based on it, this development complicated even further the already perplexing undertaking of translating the Hebrew term. The situation with finding a Greek equivalent for the Tetragram was complicated by the fact that during the period under discussion, oral usage of the Ineffable Name had already become extremely limited.[8] Thus, two functional forms co-existed: the original written but now tabooed form, alongside various Hebrew and Aramaic substitutions.[9] As was formulated later, "I am not pronounced as I am written" (*b. Kidd.* 71a). Therefore, the Greek word could render not the Tetragram itself, but its substitutions in Hebrew and possibly Aramaic (*adonai,*

---

8 For a recent and detailed survey of research on the disuse of the Tetragram, see Anthony R. Meyer, *The Divine Name in Early Judaism: Use and Non-Use in Aramaic, Hebrew, and Greek* (PhD diss., McMaster University, 2017) 13–41. See also Guy G. Stroumsa, "A Nameless God: Judaeo-Christian and Gnostic 'Theologies of the Name,' " in *The Image of the Judeo-Christians in Ancient Jewish and Christian Literature: Papers Delivered at the Colloquium of the Institutum Iudaicum, Brussels, 18–19 November 2001* (ed. Peter J. Tomson and Doris Lambers-Petry; Tübingen: Mohr Siebeck, 2003) 230–43; Kristin De Troyer, "The Names of God, their Pronunciation and their Translation: A Digital Tour of Some of the Main Witnesses," Lectio Difficilior 2 (2005) https://www.lectio.unibe.ch/en/archive/kristin-de-troyer-the-names-of-god-their-pronunciation-and-their-translation-a-digital-tour-of-some-of-the-main-witnesses.html; eadem, "The Pronunciation of the Names of God: With Some Notes Regarding 'Nomina sacra'," in *Gott nennen: Gottes Namen und Gott als Name* (ed. Ingolf U. Dalferth and Philipp Stoellger; Religion in Philosophy and Theology 35; Tübingen: Mohr Siebeck, 2008) 143–172; Pavlos D. Vasileiadis, "The Pronunciation of the Sacred Tetragrammaton: An Overview of a *Nomen Revelatus* that Became a *Nomen Absconditus*," *Judaica Ukrainica* 2 (2013) 5–20.

9 Cf. similar substitutions in other practices, like the descriptive *Bel* (also meaning "lord") for the proper name *Marduk*. On κύριος for Greco-Roman and especially Oriental deities and on numeric substitutions of divine names, see below.

mara(n), ribbon, shema, etc.). Since the meanings and connotations of both forms of representation—both original and substitutional—were relevant in Semitic usage, both had to be taken into account when translating to Greek.

3 Lost in translation

It was, of course, an impossible task to translate this Hebrew name. The Greek term inevitably failed to express most of the diverse elements of content contained not only in the Tetragram itself but even in its most common Semitic substitutions.[10] However, the incongruity of Greek equivalents was much more striking in relation to the Tetragram itself. It is not surprising that some Greek translators simply gave up on the challenge and kept the Hebrew word intact (sometimes in paleo-Hebrew script) or even left an empty space (into which the Hebrew word was probably supposed to be written later).

Compared to the Hebrew Tetragram, Greek κύριος provides a functional description instead of a name (and thus, contributes rather to theology than mythology). However, in addition to bringing new opportunities for theologizing the term in certain respects,[11] it also brought theological constriction and the loss of a wider exegetical perspective. This is because the Greek term lacked a number of the Tetragram's semantic and functional characteristics, such as: a) verbal meaning; b) the quality of a proper name; c) uniqueness; and, moreover, its d) phonetic, e) graphic, and f) numeric values. Before introducing our new analysis here (which relates mainly to the last point), it is important to demonstrate what pains ancient Judeo-Greek[12] translators were prepared to take in order to overcome these deficiencies and to preserve at least some of the characteristics of the Tetragram that could easily be lost in translation. These include:

a) *Verbal meaning.* The Tetragram's verbal meaning of "be" or "cause to be," actualized in the Hebrew texts of Ex 3:14 and Hos 1:9, was lost in κύριος and other equivalents. However, it found actualization in the substantivized participle ὁ ὤν (or τὸ ὄν) "the One who is / the Being," which translated אהיה (אשר) in LXX Ex 3:14. This term was frequently used as God's name by Philo (*Abr.* 107, 119–123, esp. 121; *Det.* 160, *Mut.* 11–13, *Som.* 1.231–4). This Judeo-Platonic term was also appropriated

---

10 Such as plurality and the possessive form of *adonai* "my lords."

11 See, e.g., the discussion in George Howard, "The Tetragram and the New Testament," *Journal of Biblical Literature* 96.1 (1977) 63–83, and the references there.

12 Hereafter we use the term Judeo-Greek mostly in an inclusive way, referring also to the early Christians and avoiding anachronistic dichotomy between the two groups.

34 —— Alexander Kulik

and widely used by Naassenes and other groups defined as Gnostics and possibly by the second-century pagan philosopher Numenius of Apamea.[13]

b) *Proper name.* The very existence of ancient Semitic gods was connected to their ability to be "called by name" (*Enuma Elish* 1.6–10; cf. Ex 3:13).[14] This entire sphere of "Name" mythology and mysticism would be lost with the substitution of a descriptive title for a *nomen proprium.* Knowing the name is a religious value (Ps 9:11; 91:14). God's name is "on" his messenger (Ex 23:21). The name can be loved (Ps 5:11), praised (7:17; 9:2), and trusted (20:7); it can protect a person (20:1). God's name is in fact his very presence (Deut 12:5; 1 Kg 8:6 *et pass.*). Some verses, in fact, do not make sense unless the proper name is meant (Ex 6:3; Isa 42:8; Jer. 16:21; Ps 83:18). The fact of its existence and magic powers was known also to learned Greek pagan and Christian authors.[15]

c) *Uniqueness.* The Hebrew version of the Name was not only personal, but also unique. The Greek equivalent was anything but unique and could bear other religious and profane meanings: from deities and demons to worldly rulers and "masters" in the widest spectrum of senses related to ownership of property and slaves, authority over disciples, or even polite address. Thus, in addition to losing some original meanings of the Semitic surrogates of the Tetragram, the Greek title gained new meanings absent in the original forms. This profane-sacral polysemy of κύριος enabled cases of confusion or intentional play among the meanings of "master",[16]

---

13 See A. Marmorstein, "Philo and the Names of God," *Jewish Quarterly Review* 22.3 (1932) 295–306; N. A. Dahl and A. F. Segal, "Philo and the Rabbis on the Names of God," *Journal for the Study of Judaism* 9.2 (1978) 1–28; Gerard. P. Luttikhuizen, "The Revelation of the Unknowable God in Coptic Gnostic Texts," in *The Revelation of the Name YHWH to Moses: Perspectives from Judaism, the Pagan Graeco-Roman World, and Early Christianity* (ed. G. H. van Kooten, R. A. Kugler, and L. T. Stuckenbruck; Leiden: Brill, 2007) 237–246; Robert J. Wilkinson, *Tetragrammaton: Western Christians and the Hebrew Name of God from the Beginnings to the Seventeenth Century* (Studies in the History of Christian Traditions 179; Leiden: Brill, 2016) 158–159.

14 "When no gods whatever had been brought into being, uncalled by name, their destinies undetermined. Then it was that the gods were formed within them. Lahmu and Lahamu were brought forth, by name they were called" (Enuma Elish 1.7–10; *The Ancient Near Eastern Texts Relating to the Old Testament* [ed. James Bennett Pritchard; 3rd ed.; ANET 60–61; Princeton: Princeton University Press, 1969] 60–61).

15 G. H. van Kooten, "Moses/Musaeus/Mochos and his God Yahweh, Iao, and Sabaoth, Seen from a Graeco-Roman Perspective," in *Revelation of the Name*, 107–138. On magic powers of the Hebrew Name, see Morton Smith, *Jesus the Magician* (San Francisco: Harper and Row, 1978) 49; Hans-Jürgen Becker, "The Magic of the Name and Palestinian Rabbinic Literature," in *The Talmud Yerushalmi and Graeco-Roman Culture* (ed. Peter Schäfer; 3 vols.; Texte und Studien zum antiken Judentum 71, 79, 93; Tübingen: Mohr Siebeck, 1998–2002) 3:391–407; Gideon Bohak, *Ancient Jewish Magic: A History* (Cambridge: Cambridge University Press, 2008) 117–19, 198–201, 305–7; 376–78.

16 Including in the rabbinic Hebrew loan form (ס)קיר in both profane and sacral meanings.

"teacher",[17] "king," and "divine being." Even uniquely biblical combinations of divine titles did not always help to differentiate God from his creatures in Greek. This situation could and did cause certain confusions for religious thought. When applied to Jesus, this enabled his assimilation with God and had consequences for the emergence of binitarian and trinitarian theology.[18]

d) *Phonetic value.* Despite the tendency to taboo oral usage of the Name, its phonetic form was transcribed into Greek as ιαω and other similar forms.[19] This Greek transcription of the Hebrew form possibly gave impetus to the development of a new theological and rhetorical device in Revelation: "I am the Alpha and the Omega"—the two letters adjacent in ιαω (1:8; 21:6; 22:13).

e) *Graphic value.* Another extreme was furnished by graphic imitation of the Hebrew letters by means of visually similar Greek ones (ΠΙΠΙ), as witnessed *inter alia* by Jerome (*Ep. 25 ad Marcellum*).[20]

f) *Numeric value.* Based on the information presented heretofore, one may receive the impression that Jewish Greek literati, while going to great lengths to express diverse meanings and features of the Tetragram, totally neglected only one aspect: its numeric value (*yod-heh-vav-heh*, 10+5+6+5=26). Is this likely?

One way to address this question would be to consider it superfluous: *the Tetragram did not have a numeric value* at the time when its Greek equivalents were introduced, because Jews did not assign numeric values to their letters until a relatively late period. Hebrew-Greek translations started in the third century BCE, while Hebrew alphabetic numerals are not attested before the late second century BCE.

This answer cannot satisfy for the following reasons. Not only did the search for equivalents of the Tetragram not cease in the later period, after Hebrew alphabetic numerals had been documented (and in fact, our data primarily pertains to this later period), but furthermore, indirect evidence of Hebrew alphabetic numerals exists from an earlier era. Since the late 1980s a series of works have appeared that lend more weight to numerical criticism of the Bible and cannot help but explain various phenomena in the biblical content and structure through means

---

17 As in Hebrew and Aramaic *rabbi, maran(a), rabboni.*

18 Additional consequences, not all of them purely theological, also ensued, such as martyrdom for refusing to call emperors κύριος. See, e.g., Dalman, *Gottesname*, 326–30; A. Deissman, *Light from the Ancient East* (New York, 1927) 357–61.

19 See the list of possible Greek transcriptions of the Tetragram assembled by Vasileiadis ("Pronunciation," 77–82).

20 CSEL 54.219. See *Monumenta Sacra et Profana VII Codex Syro-Hexaplaris Ambrosianus* (ed. A. M. Ceriani; London, 1874), 1.106–12; C. Taylor, *Hebrew-Greek Cairo Genizah Palimpsests* (Cambridge, 1900) 6–11; Wilkinson, *Tetragrammaton*, 89–96, 72–74.

other than isopsephy. Parallel phenomena have also been found in other Semitic sources, which are likewise unequivocally independent from the Greek tradition. As a result, Mesopotamian origins of isopsephy and associated numerological techniques have been proposed.[21] It is noteworthy that the majority of supposed cases of biblical isopsephism are based on the number 26, a numeric representation of the name of God:[22]

– beatitudes (אשרי formulae) are found 26 times in Psalms;[23]
– the refrain "for his grace is forever" is repeated 26 times in Ps 136;[24]
– Genesis 49:2–27 (Jacob's blessings) contains 26 verses;[25]
– Deut 5:14 (the commandment to observe the seventh day) contains 26 words;[26]
– Deut 32:1–3 ("Exordium," the introductory passage of the Song of Moses) contains 26 words;[27]
– Deut 33:2–3 (on the appearance of God) contains 26 words;[28] etc.

The numerological significance of 26 can be observed also in the NT: in the usage of the Johannine "I am" (*ego eimi*) sayings, which identify Jesus with the "Father." This phrase is unique to Jewish Greek texts and is thought to render the Hebrew אני הוא found in passages such as Deut 32:39 and Isa 48:1. In a manner similar to the

---

21 See Lieberman, "Mesopotamian Background," 186–92; Jacob Bazak, "The Geometric-Figurative Structure of Psalm CXXXVI," *VT* 35 (1985) 129–38; idem, "Numerical Devices in Biblical Poetry," *VT* 38 (1988) 333–37; Casper Labuschagne, "Significant Compositional Techniques in the Psalms: Evidence for the Use of Number as an Organizing Principle," *VT* 59 (2009) 583–605; Israel Knohl, "Sacred Architecture: The Numerical Dimensions of Biblical Poems," *VT* 62.2 (2012) 189-197; idem, "Solving the Mystery of Genesis 49:10b? The Numerical Key," *VT* 70.3 (2020) 499–501; Tzahi Weiss, *Letters by which Heaven and Earth Were Created: The Origins and the Meanings of the Perceptions of Alphabetic Letters as Independent Units in Jewish Sources of Late Antiquity* (Jerusalem: Mosad Bialik, 2014) 25–30, 33–35 (in Hebrew).
22 Labuschagne, "Significant Compositional Techniques," 586. See also there on the use of 17 as an alternative isopsephon for the Tetragram. On 52 as the number of weeks in a solar year, see Knohl, "Sacred Architecture," 192–3.
23 See Frank Lothar Hossfeld and Erich Zenger, *Psalms 3: A Commentary on Psalms 101–150* (Hermeneia: A Critical and Historical Commentary on the Bible; Minneapolis: Fortress Press, 2011) 398. The authors do not connect this fact to the numeric value of the Tetragram.
24 Bazak, "Geometric-Figurative Structure," 129.
25 See more in Knohl, "Solving the Mystery."
26 Claus Schedi, *Baupläne des Wortes. Einführung in die biblische Logotechnik.* Wien: Herder, 1974: 172; Labuschagne, "Significant Compositional Techniques," 592.
27 Knohl, "Sacred Architecture," 194. Knohl notes that the Exordium is the only paragraph in the Song of Moses that refers explicitly to the name of God ("For the name LORD I will proclaim," 32:3).
28 Without ויאמר (Knohl, "Sacred Architecture," 190).

patterns observed in the Hebrew Bible, it occurs precisely twenty-six times in the Gospel of John.

If we accept these calculations as meaningful and not accidental, then the symbolism of 26 would become the earliest attested case of Hebrew gematria. This might have been based solely on the numeric value of the Tetragram—which would not be surprising, given the centrality of the term for Jewish thought and religious practice.

Moreover, as this paper will demonstrate, the numeric value of the Hebrew Tetragram does appear also in Greek translations.

4 God's name as number and the origins of nomina sacra

This study suggests that the numeric value of God's name not only was not neglected but, on the contrary, was introduced with clarity for an authentic target audience.

Drawing upon the well-documented graphic identity of the Hellenistic *sigma* and *digamma* in the form of the lunate c, I will demonstrate that the *nomen sacrum* κ̄c̄, a commonly employed contracted form of κύριος, used as an equivalent of the Hebrew Tetragram, was isomorphic to the Greek alphabetic numeral κ̄c̄ (*kappa-digamma*, 20+6=26). Thus, it must have been devised as an isopsephism of the Hebrew divine name (*yod-heh-vav-heh*, 10+5+6+5=26). This suggestion aligns well with the fact that the majority of purported cases of isopsephism found in the Hebrew Bible are also based on the number 26, a numeric representation of the name of God.

The so-called "Milesian" system of Greek alphabetic numerals included three ἐπισήματα, additional characters, among which was the archaic character *digamma*, used for the numeral 6.

Already in the Classical period, this form had developed a square variant without a tail—⊏, which by the Hellenistic epoch had lost its angles to take on the rounded form C, thus making it fully homographic with the lunate *sigma*.[29]

---

[29] Thus L. H. Jeffery, *The Local Scripts of Archaic Greece* (Oxford, 1961) 23–25. The form became very common, at least outside Attica (Marcus N. Tod, "The Alphabetic Numeral System in Attica," *Annual of the British School at Athens* 45 [1950] 126–39, at 135). For the lunate sigma, see the paleographic tables in Victor E. Gardthausen, *Griechische Paläographie* (2 vols.; 2nd ed.; Leipzig, 1911–13) 2:Taf. 1–4.

This frequent graphic identity of the numeric digamma and the sigma is known to paleographers and corroborated by Graeco-Egyptian papyri.[30] I will adduce only one example out of many instances. In P.47 (Dublin, Chester Beatty Library, CBL BP III),[31] a manuscript of Revelation dating from the third century, in 9:13–14 the number 6 appears twice. In Rev 13:18 the number 6 appears as part of 666. And finally, in the same manuscript κύριος as κ̄c̄ is found in Rev 11:8. In all these cases, the number C (6) is undistinguishable from the letter C (σ).

Thus, κ̄c̄, the main Greek equivalent of the Tetragram, the most common contracted form of κύριος, could be completely indistinguishable from the Greek numeral κ̄c̄ (26), the numeric value of the Tetragram in Hebrew. These two forms were perfect homographs.

Two additional factors further enhanced their identity:

a) The contracted form of abbreviation, in which only the initial and final letters of a word are denoted—in contrast to suspension, in which the end of the word is omitted (as in κ̄ῡ for κύ[ριος])—was not known in this period outside Jewish/Christian-Greek texts. It must have been a Hellenistic Jewish innovation imitating consonantal writing and based on early attested West Semitic practices.[32] Thus,

---

30 G. Ranocchia, "Is ϝ-shaped digamma attested as a numerical sign in Greek papyri? Once more on P.Herc. 1669 and P.Oxy. 1176," *Journal of Hellenic Studies* 140 (2020) 199–205, at 199, 202–203 (esp. n. 8), where he adduces the following examples of manuscripts with identical digamma and sigma: *P.Lond.Lit.* 28, col. 11, 42; *P.Grenf.* II 11, col. 2, 4; *P.Oxy.* 4449, col. 1 (upper margin); *P.Oxy.* 4499, *fr.* 16, 3 recto; *P.Beatty* III f. 1v, 9 and 13, f. 7r, 10; *P.Beatty* VI, f. 11r, 11 *passim.* Cf. "Das Vau hat in der älteren Papyrusschrift noch seine ursprünglichere Form C," etc. (Gardthausen, *Griechische Paläographie*, 2.265); "In NT manuscripts it [digamma] is fairly rare (most scribes tended to use the longhand ἕξ), but when it appears it sometimes takes the form C, which is visually undifferentiated from the lunate *sigma*" (Zachary J. Cole, *Numerals in Early Greek New Testament Manuscripts: Text-Critical, Scribal, and Theological Studies* [Leiden: Brill, 2017] 3). Cole also mentions several NT papyri which do not distinguish *sigma* and *digamma* (ibid., 3, 50, 64, 193). At the same time, this information has not been as easily accessible as it might have been: most popular paleographic tables, including the ones by Gardhausen, Thompson, and Harrauer, for some reason do not include the additional numeric letters (ἐπισήματα). See Edward M. Thompson, *An Introduction to Greek and Latin Palaeography* (Oxford, 1912) 144–147 ("Greek literary alphabets"), 191–194 ("Greek cursive alphabets"); Gardthausen, *Griechische Paläographie*, 2:Taf. 1–5; Hermann Harrauer, *Handbuch der griechischen Paläographie* (Bibliothek des Buchwesens 20; Stuttgart, 2010) 1:143–171 (§XII: "Bilderdatei zu den Buchstabenformen").

31 See the images: https://manuscripts.csntm.org/manuscript/Group/GA_P47.

32 See Ludwig Traube, *Nomina Sacra: Versuch einer Geschichte der christlichen Kürzung* (Munich: Beck, 1907); Thompson, Introduction, 75–78; A. Millard, "Ancient Abbreviations and the Nomina Sacra," in *The Unbroken Reed: Studies in the Culture and Heritage of Ancient Egypt in Honour of A. F. Shore* (ed. C. J. Eyre,

Naming God and Other Challenges of Transcultural Monotheism ——— **39**

when this abbreviating convention was introduced, it required a special effort to recognize it as such, whereas the numeric signification of such abbreviations would have been much more readily recognizable.

b) The identity of κ̅ς̅ as a number was enhanced by the use of a macron (supralinear horizontal stroke), while outside the Judeo/Christian-Greek tradition and its successors, the macron was utilized mainly for numerals and never for abbreviations.[33] In fact, our hypothesis positing a numeric significance of κ̅ς̅ may suggest a solution to the question of why all *nomina sacra* were presented—unusually for a general Greek reader—in this semi-numeric form. The very choice to present the name of God as a number might also lie behind the choice to use supralinear strokes for all other contracted *nomina sacra*.

Thus, outside the Jewish/Christian usages, the sign κ̅ς̅ could signify only a number and nothing else. At the same time, when found in a Jewish/Christian text it becomes (for a competent reader) both *nomen sacrum* and *numerus sacer*. "The name which cannot be expressed in words" (Irenaeus, *Haer.* 1.14.9) was thus conveyed by means of a number.

In addition to representing an original numerical value, κ̅ς̅ served additional purposes. As we have already noted, it aided in distinguishing between the sacred and profane meanings of κύριος. In early manuscripts, there is a noticeable effort to employ the contracted form for the former and the full form for the latter.[34] It becomes clear now why the abbreviated form was chosen for the divine name and the full form for the mundane usage, rather than vice versa. The association of κ̅ς̅ with the divine name went beyond mere convention: κ̅ς̅ was a form more closely related to the Tetragram than was κύριος. Furthermore, this usage also sheds new light on the possibility of early binitarian Christology, when κ̅ς̅ with its enhanced divine associations was applied to Jesus.[35]

M. A. Leahy, and L. M. Leahy; Egypt Exploration Society, Occasional publications 11; London: Egyptian Exploration Society, 1994) 221–26; A. Millard, *Reading and Writing in the Time of Jesus* (Sheffield: Sheffield Academic Press, 2001) 70–71; Charlesworth, "Consensus Standardization," 39.

33 See Larry W. Hurtado, "The Origin of the *Nomina Sacra*: A Proposal," *JBL* 117 (1998) 655–73, at 658–9, and references there (n. 11). The supralinear stroke could be used also for "words or other combinations of letters which were to be regarded as foreign or emphatic matter ... Mystic words, including the sacred names, in Egyptian Greek magical papyri are also thus marked" (Thompson, *Introduction*, 77). See also Cole: "The mechanics of abbreviating numbers were so similar to names that, apart from context, the *nomina sacra* can be at times visually indistinguishable from abbreviated numbers" (*Numerals*, 173).

34 See the section "Lost in Translation," point C (above).

35 On the high Christological hypothesis, see Martin Hengel, *The Son of God: The Origin of Christology and the History of Jewish-Hellenistic Religion* (Philadelphia: Fortress, 1976); Larry W.

5 Precedents and parallels

5.1 Other cases of Hebrew-Greek isopsephy

Greek isopsephy (the practice of adding up the number values of the letters in a word to form a single number) is known from at least the third century BCE and becomes better attested from no later than the first century CE, especially among Jews and Christians.[36] Isopsephy was, in fact, part of numerological beliefs and practices widely involved in cultic, magic/scientific, mystic, theological, and philosophical discourses starting from Pythagorean numerical mysticism and continuing through Platonic and Aristotelean number theories (which considered *inter alia* numbers as "primary causes of existing things"; Aristotle, *Met.* 13.1080a) and on to early Christian debates over the theological significance of numbers.[37]

Hurtado, *The Earliest Christian Artifacts: Manuscripts and Christian Origins* (Grand Rapids, MI: Eerdmans, 2006) 105–106; idem, "The Binitarian Shape of Early Christian Worship," in *The Jewish Roots of Christological Monotheism: Papers from the St. Andrews Conference on the Historical Origins of the Worship of Jesus* (ed. Carey C. Newman, James R. Davila, and Gladys S. Lewis; *JSJSup* 6; Leiden: Brill, 1999) 187–213; idem, *At the Origins of Christian Worship: The Context and Character of Earliest Christian Devotion* (Grand Rapids, MI: Eerdmans, 2000) 63–97; idem, *Lord Jesus Christ: Devotion to Jesus in Earliest Christianity* (Grand Rapids, MI: Eerdmans, 2004) 108–18, 134–53. On Jesus as the hypostasized Name of the Father, see *Gospel of Truth* 38; Clement, *Excerpta ex Theodoto* 22–27; Jean Daniélou, *A History of Early Christian Doctrine: The Theology of Jewish Christianity* (London, 1964, 1973) 147–163; Raoul Mortley, "The Name of the Father is the Son (Gospel of Truth 38)," in *Neoplatonism and Gnosticism* (ed. R. T. Wallis and J. Bregman; Albany, NY: SUNY Press, 1992) 239–252.

36 See, e.g., Alan Cameron, "Ancient Anagrams," *The American Journal of Philology* 116.3 (1995) 477–84; Joel Kalvesmaki, "Isopsephic Inscriptions from Iasos (Inschriften von Iasos 419) and Shnān ('IGLS' 1403)," *ZPE* 161 (2007) 261–68; J. L. Hilton, "On Isopsephic Lines in Homer and Apollonius of Rhodes," *The Classical Journal* 106.4 (2011) 385–94; Julia Lougovaya, "Isopsephisms in P.Jena II 15a-b," *ZPE 176* (2011) 200–4; Ast and Lougovaya, "Art of Isopsephism." For a parody on isopsephy see Lucian, *Alex.* 11.

37 See, e.g., Robert Eisler, *Orpheus the Fisher: Comparative Studies in Orphic and Early Christian Cult Symbolism* (London: Watkins, 1921) 115–120; Dornseiff, *Alphabet in Mystik*; Oskar Rühle, 'ἀριθμέω, ἀριθμός, *TWNT* 1 (1933) 461–4; Vincent Foster Hopper, *Medieval Number Symbolism: Its Sources, Meaning, and Influence on Thought and Expression* (Columbia University Studies in English and Comparative Literature 132; New York: Columbia University Press, 1938); O. H. Lehmann, "Number-Symbolism as a Vehicle of Religious Experience in the Gospels, Contemporary Rabbinic Literature and the Dead Sea Scrolls," *Studia Patristica* 4.2 (Texte und Untersuchungen zur Geschichte der altchristlichen Literatur 79; Berlin: Akademie, 1961) 125–35; M. H. Pope, "Number, Numbering, Numbers," *Interpreter's Dictionary of the Bible* (ed. G. A. Buttrick et al.; 5 vols.;

In the case of κͼ, we are dealing with interlinguistic isopsephy—when the numeric values of letters in one language are signified by the letters-numbers of another language and thus the numeric identity is found between the forms of different languages. Such Hebrew-Greek isopsephies are attested not earlier than the first century CE. Among the most famous are the "number of the beast" of Rev 13:18 and the numeric value of Hebrew דוד (14) lying behind the symbolism of the three sets of fourteen generations in Mt 1:17.[38] Irenaeus discussed the importance of using Hebrew ("propriam Hebraeorum linguam") and not Greek for isopsephic speculations (*Haer.* 2.24.1–2). Hebrew-Greek gematrias have been proposed for *Asc. Mos.* 9:1,[39] *3 Baruch*,[40] and one more *nomen sacrum*: the suspended abbreviation ιη for Jesus (Ἰη[σοῦς]), which is homographic to 18 (as noticed already in the *Barn.* 9:7–9 and Clement of Alexandria, *Strom.* 6.278-80). With regard to the latter, Larry Hurtado has proposed the Hebrew isopsephon חי ("alive" and 18).[41] Thus, κͼ may not be the only *nomen sacrum* homographic to a numeral with a Hebrew isopsephon.

Nashville: Abingdon, 1962) 3:561–567; Reinhart Staats, "Ogdoas als ein Symbol für die Auferstehung," *Vigiliae Christianae* 26.1 (1972) 29–52; Dominic O'Meara, *Pythagoras Revived: Mathematics and Philosophy in Late Antiquity* (Oxford: Oxford University Press, 1989); Lawrence P. Schrenk, "God as Monad: The Philosophical Basis of Medieval Theological Numerology," in *Medieval Numerology* (ed. Robert L. Surles; Garland Reference Library of the Humanities 1640; Garland Medieval Casebooks 7; New York: Garland, 1996) 3–10; O. Neugebauer and G. Saliba, "On Greek Numerology," *Centaurus* 31.3 (1988); J. Friberg, "Numbers and Counting," in Anchor Bible Dictionary (ed. David N. Freedman; 6 vols.; New York: Doubleday, 1992) 4:1139–46; Adela Yarbro Collins, "Numerical Symbolism in Jewish and Early Christian Apocalyptic Literature," in her *Cosmology and Eschatology in Jewish and Christian Apocalypticism* (Supplements to the Journal for the Study of Judaism 50; Leiden: Brill, 1996) 55–138; Francois Bovon, "Names and Numbers in Early Christianity," *NTS* 47 (2001) 267–88; Mikeal C. Parsons, "'Exegesis by the Numbers': Numerology and the New Testament," *Perspectives in Religious Studies* 35 (2008) 25–43; Joel Kalvesmaki, *Theology of Arithmetic: Number Symbolism in Platonism and Early Christianity* (Hellenic Studies 59; Washington, D.C.: Center for Hellenic Studies, 2013); Cole, *Numerals*.

38 On the latter, see, e.g., Hurtado, *Earliest Christian Artifacts*, 114; Cole, *Numerals*, 190.

39 Edna Israeli, " 'Taxo' and the Origin of the 'Assumption of Moses,' " *JBL* 128.4 (2009) 735–57.

40 Gideon Bohak, "Greek-Hebrew Gematrias in 3 Baruch and in Revelation," *JSP* 7 (1990) 119–21; Alexander Kulik, *3 Baruch: Greek-Slavonic Apocalypse of Baruch* (Commentaries on Early Jewish Literature; Berlin: de Gruyter, 2010) 59, 226.

41 Hurtado, "Origin," 665–69; idem, *Earliest Christian Artifacts*, 115–17; cf. Cole, *Numerals*, 180–184. These Hebrew and Greek forms are also similar graphically (cf. the discussion of ΠΙΙΙΙ above and the graphical identity of the names of gods and numbers in Mesopotamian cuneiform documents below). See also a connected case of Christian numeric symbolism in another *numerus sacer* — τιη (318 = *tau* as a depiction of a cross with ιη "Jesus") applied to the number 318 as found in Gen 14:14 (*Barn.* 9:8; Lieberman, "Mesopotamian Background," 168–9; Hurtado, "Origin," 666–667;

5.2 Other names-numbers: nomina sacra as numeri sacri

The *nomen sacrum* k͞c represents a widely attested phenomenon, that of the *name-number*, which is observed most often with the names of deities. The focus on the numeric value of God's name in Hebrew—and, more especially, the complete identity of God's name and number in the *numerus sacer/nomen sacrum* k͞c—should be regarded in the context of the graphic identity of the names of gods with other numbers attested in Mesopotamian cuneiform documents (from the eighth-century BCE Akkadian to the second-century BCE Parthian). For instance: the sign of the moon god Sin was identical to the number 30; the name of the sun god Shamash, to the number 20; Enlil, the head of the Sumerian pantheon of gods, to 50; Igigi, the word for great gods of heaven and earth, to 600; et cetera.[42] This is not yet isopsephy, since numeric value is assigned to whole words instead of letters or their combinations, but the result is the same: meaningful *homography of gods' names and signs for numbers.*

Greek isopsephy is applied most often to proper names.[43] The Pythagorean tradition associated numbers with gods,[44] so it is no wonder that these isopsephic names often belong to gods, like Isis (420), Sarapis (662),[45] and deified Roman

---

idem, *Earliest Christian Artifacts*, 114–15, and the references in n. 59 there; Cole, *Numerals*, 178–184). On ι͞η as presumably the earliest *nomen sacrum*, see *Fragments of an Unknown Gospel and Other Early Christian Papyri* (ed. H. I. Bell and T. C. Skeat; London: Trustees of the British Museum, 1935) 3–4; Roberts, *Manuscript*, 37; Hurtado, "Origin," 665–66.

42 Discussed by Steven Lieberman as corroboration of the early existence of Hebrew isopsephy ("A Mesopotamian Background," 174–76, 187–88, 199; see there also on Mandaean number-based names; E. S. Drower, *The Mandaeans of Iraq and Iran* [Oxford: Clarendon, 1937] 81–82). Names in the form of longhand ordinal numbers are well known in Latin (like Quintus, Octavia, and many others) as well as in Coptic, Armenian, and Syriac.

43 David E. Aune, *Revelation 6–16* (Word Biblical Commentary 52b; Nashville: Nelson, 1998) 772. See more examples in Ast and Lougovaya, "Art of Isopsephism." Cf. Francois Bovon: "The early Christians used the categories of 'name' and 'number' as theological tools. Often they consciously interpreted names and numbers in a symbolic way. Even their non-reflexive usage relied on implicit conceptualizations very different from our nominalist-based thinking. They presupposed that names and numbers are inextricably related. Is the Jewish and Christian confession εἷς ὁ θεὸς not a cogent expression combining a name and a number?" ("Names and Numbers in Early Christianity," *NTS* 47 (2001) 267–88, at 267; see there also about the "kinship between signs for words and signs for numbers" on p. 276).

44 P. Gorman, *Pythagoras* (London: Routledge, 1979) 151.

45 P. Oxy. XLV 3239 (late 2nd cent. CE), l. 21 and 31: Ἶσις [420] ὁ Σαρᾶπις [662] ἡ μεγάλη [ἐ]λπίς ["the great hope"; 420], Ἀλεξάνδρειαν κοσμεῖ ["adorns Alexandria"; 662] (Ast and Lougovaya, "Art

Naming God and Other Challenges of Transcultural Monotheism — **43**

emperors.[46] The deity Abrasax (Abraxas) is addressed by its isopsephonic number τξε (365).[47] The name of Mithras as well was known to Jerome as an isopsephon of the same solaric number.[48]

Christians applied similar numerological practices to their deified figures. Numbers could substitute for the name of Jesus, who was called ἐπίσημον (a letter for 6)—because "Jesus is a name arithmetically symbolical, consisting of six letters" (*Haer.* 1.14.4–7; cf. 2.24.1; Hippolytus, *Ref.* 6.40, 44)—or titled by its isopsephon 888 (ibid. 2.24.1; cf. 1.15.5; *Syb. Oracles* 1.324–31). The Holy Spirit's symbolic representation, a dove, Greek περιστερά, was known as an isopsephon of ϣα (801; *Haer.* 1.14.6). The contracted form of Ἰη[σοῦς]), the *nomen sacrum* ιη̄, could also be understood as the number 18 (*Barn.* 9:7–9; Clement of Alexandria, *Strom.* 6.11; see above), etc.

6 Conclusions

It can hardly have been a coincidence that the *nomen sacrum* κ̄ς̄, a perfect isomorph of the Greek number κ̄ς̄ (26), became the main equivalent of the Hebrew Tetragram which has the very same numeric value. What remains is the question of how to date this phenomenon.

Most of our knowledge concerning Hellenistic Judaism comes through Christian hands, and it is often difficult, if not impossible, to distinguish pre-Christian Jewish heritage preserved in Christian sources from original creativity confined to Christian groups. Therefore, the observations presented in this paper may be interpreted in at least two ways:

(1) κ̄ς̄ could be a Hellenistic Jewish innovation that devised an inventive way to connect the widely used κύριος to a numeric value of the Tetragram. An even bolder theory would assert the precedence of κ̄ς̄ to the term's full form, thus

---

of Isopsephy," 94). Sarapis appears also in the 4th-cent. *Historia Alexandri Magni* of Pseudo-Callisthenes, where the god presents himself to the king as a list of numeric values of his name's letters: "Listen, Alexander, to who I am: two times one hundred and a one put together, then another hundred and one, four times twenty and ten, then take the first letter and put it also last, and then you will know which god I am" (I.33.11.37–41; Ast and Lougovaya, "Art of Isopsephy," 84–85).

46 There are multiple examples from the *Sibylline Oracles* as well as Nero in Revelation (13:18) and Suetonius (*Vitae*, Nero 39.2).

47 Ἀβρασάξ or Ἀβράξας (*PGM* [*Papyri Graecae Magicae*] 8.61; Ast and Lougovaya, "Art of Isopsephy," 89).

48 Jerome, *Comm. in Am.* 1.3.9–10 (*CCL* [*Corpus Christianorum*, Series Latina] 76.250).

explaining the very choice of κύριος by numerological considerations. In other words, κ̄ς̄ could have been initially and intentionally devised by early Jewish translators in order to preserve the numeric value of the Tetragram in Greek. In this case, we would be justified in regarding κ̄ς̄ as a relic of an original Jewish tradition that a) introduced the Semitic mode of contraction (instead of Greek suspension), b) used with such contraction the Greek mode of presenting numbers (with a macron), and c) chose κύριος for the name of God—all in order to preserve the numeric value of the Hebrew Tetragram. Preserved by Christians, κ̄ς̄ was imitated in their new names-numbers, such as ῑς̄. These could have been modeled after it or devised independently, based on the same graphic phenomenon. This interpretation has the advantage of explaining why nomina sacra were presented in a numeric form.

(2) Alternatively, as it is unknown to early manuscripts or inscriptions that are undoubtedly Jewish, κ̄ς̄ might have been just one of the Christian names-numbers that are attested in Christian sources of the second and third centuries CE. κ̄ς̄ could possibly even be secondary to π̄ and ῑς̄ and imitate their numeric isomorphism. However, even if a Christian invention, κ̄ς̄, being based on Hebrew isopsephism, must have belonged to the early Jewish-Christian community.

Whether κύριος and/or *nomina sacra* including κ̄ς̄ were originally Jewish preChristian or were introduced by Christians, it is now evident that the distinction between the profane and sacred meanings of κύριος through the use of its full and contracted forms was not merely a convention but a consequence of the contracted form's closer association with the Tetragram. Furthermore, due to the same association, the application of κ̄ς̄ to Jesus and the consistent effort to differentiate it from κύριος in the mundane sense, as attested in early manuscripts, may have played an even more significant role in early Christian binitarianism than is usually attributed to κύριος, thus potentially tilting the balance in favor of the early high Christological hypothesis.

Elisabeth Gräb-Schmidt

The Anthropological Turn of Religion – Towards a Paradigm Shift in Transcendence References in Modernity

In the course of secularisation, it was now necessary either to abandon religion or to assign it a new place.[1] Some see this as a confirmation of the indispensability of religion, while others see therein only a rebellion and a temporary return of it. For both positions on the relationship between religion and secularisation however, it was clear that from now on religion had to prove its legitimacy in the forum of reason.

This makes it all the more challenging to ask what religion is actually about and what is meant by religion. Although some representatives want to dispense with a definition due to the disparate nature of the phenomena[2], there are various attempts to define religion, from the specialist for transcendence to the system-theoretical explanation, according to which religion is responsible for the 'administration of immanence – transcendence difference', or quite simply that it is understood as a 'cultural system' "that provides answers to questions such as: where do we come from? Where are we going to? What is the meaning of it all?"[3]. And if you define religion in this way, then you can assume that there is no society that does not possess this form of religion in some way, i.e. that it develops institutions that provide answers and regulate how these questions have to be dealt with.

The examination of the definition of religion always also applies to the problem addressed by the secularisation thesis. This became a central element of self-understanding in the 20th century, at least among European intellectuals.[4] In its

---

[1] Michael Bergunder, "Was ist Religion? Kulturwissenschaftliche Überlegungen zum Gegenstand der Religionswissenschaft," *Zeitschrift für Religionswissenschaft* 19 (2011/1): 3–55. Cf. Elisabeth Gräb-Schmidt, "Abschied von der Säkularisierungsthese," *ZThK* 110 (2013): 74–108.

[2] Detlef Pollack, *Handbuch Religionssoziologie* (Wiesbaden: Springer VS, 2018).

[3] Cf. the Voices of Thomas M. Schmidt, Knut Wenzel, Ferdinand Sutterlüthy und Richard Traunmüller, Rolf Wiggershaus, "Vier Frankfurter Professoren über Religion und Gesellschaft," *Forschung Frankfurt. Das Wissenschaftsmagazin der Goethe-Universität* (2016/1): 11–15, 12. (Cf. Richard Traunmüller, "Religiöse Diversität und Sozialintegration im internationalen Vergleich," *Kölner Zeitschrift für Soziologie und Sozialpsychologie* 65 (2013): 437–465.)

[4] Early representatives were Emile Durkheim, Max Weber, Hans Blumenberg (see annotations 8, 9 and 13).

∂ Open Access. © 2025 the author(s), published by De Gruyter. This work is licensed under the Creative Commons Attribution 4.0 International License.
https://doi.org/10.1515/9783112218907-004

strictest form, the secularisation thesis states that an unstoppable, irreversible and universal process of rationalisation is accompanied by the marginalisation of religion, even to the point of its disappearance.[5]

However, the theory of secularisation is no longer advocated in this form.[6] As early as the zenith of the Enlightenment, this idea was negated by Friedrich Daniel Ernst Schleiermacher, who in his speeches on religion to the educated among their detractors (Cultured Despisers) advocated the indispensability of religion for the human as an individual and for society, thus paving the way for an anthropological turn in the understanding of religion.[7]

My thesis is:

The anthropological turn of religion is understood in this article as the paradigm shift that the object of religion is not God, but human's reference to transcendence. Religion's power of orientation no longer lies simply in the authority of a higher power, God, but is established in the transcendence of the human being. By reaching out to the wholeness of life and thus being able to illuminate meaning in this life in all its fragmentariness, it gains both an epistemological and an action-theoretical function.

This thesis of the determination of religion in and as a reference to transcendence of the human and thus the anthropological turn of religion in its consequence of the epistemological and action-theoretical function of the reference to transcendence will be developed in 4 steps. First, the relationship between religion and reason in the course of the Enlightenment and modernity is traced, which is accompanied by the paradigm shift of the anthropological turn in religion. The consequence of this paradigm shift is that religion must place itself in relation to secularisation. However, by characterising religion as a reference to transcendence, a hermeneutical reference can be made that can avoid the one-sidedness of secularisation, especially the secularisation thesis, which assumed the disappearance of religion. Under the assumption of the anthropological turn,

---

5 Christiane Frey, Uwe Hebekus, David Martyn, eds., *Säkularisierung. Grundlagentexte zur Theoriegeschichte* (Berlin: Suhrkamp Verlag, 2020); Jürgen Habermas, Josef Ratzinger, *Dialektik der Säkularisierung. Über Vernunft und Religion* (Freiburg: Herder Verlag, 2018).

6 Cf. Charles Taylor, *A Secular Age* (Cambridge: The Belknap Press of Harvard University Press, 2007); Karl Gabriel, Christel Gärtner, eds., *Umstrittene Säkularisierung, Soziologische und historische Analysen zur Differenzierung von Religion und Politik* (Berlin: Berlin University Press, 2012); Detlef Pollack *Säkularisierung – ein moderner Mythos?* (Tübingen: Mohr Siebeck, 2003).

7 Cf. Friedrich Daniel Ernst Schleiermacher, *Über die Religion, Reden an die Gebildeten unter ihren Verächtern (1799)*, in *Schriften aus der Berliner Zeit 1769–1799*, vol. I/2, ed. Günter Meckenstock, *Kritische Gesamtausgabe*, (Berlin: De Gruyter, 1984), 185–326.

adherence to religion does not necessarily mean a relapse into pre-modernity, neither does it entail a regression to pre-modernity. Rather, by accepting secularisation in the anthropological turn, religion becomes an indispensable instrument for assuring the freedom and maturity of the enlightened subject. In Part 2, this process, which lies in the anthropological turn of religion in its emancipative consequences, which can emerge in the relationship between secularisation and religion, is exemplified by the important theologian and late contemporary of Kant, Friedrich Daniel Ernst Schleiermacher, who – in dialogue with Kant – turned to the determination of religion as the influence of transcendence in a way that extends beyond metaphysical critique. By fully embracing the paradigm shift of an anthropological turn, and, following Kant's line but also critically distancing himself from it, Schleiermacher unfolds a modern program of the enduring significance of religion. His model can be inspiring for current debates on religion and secularization in modernity and postmodernity.

Third, the contemporary relevance of this paradigm shift results not least from the fact that it can be used to demonstrate the human being's reference to transcendence as one that does not necessarily have to be accompanied by explicit forms of institutional religion, but can be found implicitly in a variety of life contexts. Such a broad concept of religion as a reference to transcendence is therefore open to a diversity of phenomena, as can correspond to the 'fait religieux' indicated by Jean Delumeau[8]. Fourth, this diversity of phenomena can also address the question of the plurality of religions or religious phenomena[9], which can cast a critical light on the one-sidedness of the European secularisation thesis[10]. For in these religious figures, which are also implicit, the unfulfilled, the unavailable of an irreducible ground, an uncatchable reason, is revealed in the individual, which can thus simultaneously point to a possible perspectivity and plurality-promoting function of religion. A prerequisite for such a pluralistic and emancipative understanding of religion, however, is that the individual remains thematically orientated towards himself and thus towards understanding reality in general, i.e. his relationship to the world and to himself, in an undisguised way.

---

8 Cf. Jean Delumeau, *Des Religions et des Hommes* (Paris: Desclée de Brouwer, 1997). Jean Delumeau, "Histoire des mentalités réligieuses,1975–1994," *L'annuaire du Collège de France* 108 (2008): 865–866.

9 Cf. José Casanova, *Public Religion in the modern world* (Chicago: University Press of Chicago, 1994).

10 Cf. Martin Riesebrodt, *Die Rückkehr der Religionen* (München: C.H. Beck, 2000).

1 The Shift in the Relationship between Religion and Reason in the Enlightenment and Modernity and the Challenge for Religion in the Present

In Europe, we live in the tradition of the Enlightenment, which has brought about secularisation. Secularisation is interpreted in various ways. Previously seen primarily as an anti-religious movement, European secularisation initially simply meant the disempowerment of Christian churches and their theology. This subsequently led to a loss of relevance for religion on a broad scale. This is also reconstructed by Jürgen Habermas recently in his *History of Philosophy*, in which he reflects on his own change in attitude towards religion[11]. But the secularisation thesis, which prophesied the disappearance of religion as a relic of outdated ideas, is now seen as a one-sided view.

One thing is clear: In the Age of Enlightenment, the relationship between reason and religion became the subject of discussion. Included in this new modelling of humanity's relationship to the world is the fact that religion is no longer, as it once was, the cultural background of humanity's self-understanding of being within the world. This integration of reason into a whole, a superordinate entity, was still taken for granted in antiquity and the Middle Ages; in antiquity through metaphysics and ontology, and in the Middle Ages through theology, which, so to speak, encompassed metaphysics and ontology as ontotheology, thus including the idea of nature in the sense of cosmological order or natural law. However, it was broken open in modern times, and in the name of modern rationality this break was completed at the zenith of the Enlightenment. In the course of secularisation, the ratiocentrism resulting from this rupture emerged as a new intellectual-historical model for explaining the world and the self.

Thus, there is a wide range in the debate as to how the relationship between religion and secularisation should be understood, whether the relationship is initially seen as a dissolution, as with the early Habermas, who later however, after his change in thinking about religion, as indicated by the 2001 speech Faith and Knowledge[12], no longer assumed an equation of modern society with seculari-

---

11 Cf. Jürgen Habermas, *Die okzidentale Konstellation von Glauben und Wissen*, vol. 1 of *Auch eine Geschichte der Philosophie* (Frankfurt a.M.: Suhrkamp Verlag, 2019), 79–80.
12 Cf. Jürgen Habermas, "Glaube und Wissen. Friedenspreisrede 2001," in *Zeitdiagnosen. Zwölf Essays*, ed. Jürgen Habermas (Frankfurt a.M.: Suhrkamp Verlag, 2003): 249–262.

sation, but rather a coexistence of secularisation and religious convictions.[13] Max Weber's dictum of the 'demystification of modernity' must therefore be contradicted. According to Weber's interpretation, modern rationality aimed at world domination and it was actually made possible by the disenchantment of the world (Entzauberung der Welt)[14] by Western Christianity. The total rationalisation of both, worldview and lifestyle, had in turn the consequence that religion was relegated to the irrational. The fact that it seemed to lose importance in the public consciousness in the long term seemed to confirm the secularisation thesis. That, however, is proving to be at least one-sided. This is indicated in particular by the new growth and spread of various religions, and the existence of traditional religions has at the same also revealed this questioning of the secularisation thesis since the turn of the millennium.[15] In this form at least it has a Eurocentric bias. For José Casanova therefore, in his 1994 study on Public Religion in the Modern World[16], a variety of secularisations is acknowledged, he emphasised, and not just in the European world, which only considers the Enlightenment. According to him, European modernity must learn to deal appropriately with the global challenges of increasing religious pluralism.[17]

Nevertheless, the critical relationship between rationality and transcendence, anticipated and challenged by secularisation, represents a rupture in thinking about the relationship between reason and religion that still needs to be addressed today. With Hartmut von Sass one may ask whether secularisation truly signifies the loss of the religious or a decline of the religious, or whether it is rather a transformative process that encompasses religion. This idea is supported by the fact that particularly in the German Enlightenment, the critique of religion was not about abandoning religion but illuminating its significance, unlike in France, where radical criticism of religion was presented by the circle around the Encyclopédistes and Voltaire, or in England by David Hume.[18] These different lines show already at the beginning of modernity that enlightenment is not synony-

---

13 Ibid.

14 Cf. Max Weber, "Politik als Beruf," in Geistige Arbeit als Beruf. Vier Vorträge vor dem Freistudentischen Bund. Zweiter Vortrag (München: Duncker und Humblot, 1919).

15 Cf. Wilhelm Gräb, "Auf den Spuren der Religion. Notizen zur Lage und Zukunft der Kirche," in ZEE 39 (1995): 43–56, see especially 43.

16 Cf. José Casanova, *Public Religion in the modern world* (Chicago: University Press of Chicago, 1994).

17 Ibid.

18 Cf. Ulrich Barth, "Was ist Religion? Sinndeutung zwischen Erfahrung und Letztbegründung," in *Religion in der Moderne*, ed. Ulrich Barth (Tübingen: Mohr Siebeck, 2003): 3–29.

mous with criticism of religion, as is now again asserted with old arguments by the so-called "New Atheism"[19]. There, one also encounters phenomena of transformation, when, for example, New Atheism is surprised by demands to claim religion for one's own atheistic attitude, as Ronald Dworkin, the liberal jurist and legal philosopher, attempted in his book "Religion without God"[20]. He simultaneously claims to be an atheist, but nonetheless a religious person. He wants to establish a new form of good faith that propagates a "religious atheism". Its conceptual definition can be summarized by Dworkin as follows:

> Religion is a deep, distinct, and comprehensive worldview: it holds that inherent, objective value permeates everything that the universe and its creatures are awe-inspiring that human life has purpose and the universe order. A belief in a god is only one possible manifestation or consequence of that deeper worldview. Of course, gods have served many human purposes: they have promised an afterlife, explained storms, and taken sides against enemies. But a central part of their appeal has been their supposed achievement of filling the world with value and purpose. The conviction that a god underwrites value, however, as I will argue, presupposes a prior commitment to the independent reality of that value. That commitment is available to nonbelievers as well. So theists share a commitment with some atheists that is more fundamental than what divides them, and that shared faith might therefore furnish a basis for improved communication between them. The familiar stark divide between people of religion and without religion is too crude. Many millions of people who count themselves as atheists have convictions and experiences similar to and just as profound as those that believers count as religious. They say that though they do not believe in a 'personal' god, they nevertheless believe in a 'force' in the universe 'greater than we are.'[21]

The development of such interpretations of religion seems to me to be relevant for the plausibility of the scope and transformative processes of religious-theoretical phenomena, not least because they coincide with the self-understanding of the Enlightenment, not only negating religion, but also providing a qualified definition of religion. Since the Enlightenment, criticism and affirmation of religion have gone hand in hand. This can illustrate the presence of religious plurality today.

This is mainly discovered through so-called post-secularisation, which does not reject secularisation, but rather regards it as multifaceted and complex, including the return of the religious in a pluralistic perspective, which can agree

---

19 Cf. Richard Dawkins, *The God Delusion* (London: Bantam Press, 2006); Chris Hedges, *When Atheism becomes Religion. America's New Fundamentalists* (New York City: Free Press, 2009).
20 Cf. Ronald Dworkin, *Religion without God* (Harvard: Harvard University Press, 2013).
21 Ibid., Introduction, 1f.

with a diversity of religion that was announced with the "multiple modernities" named by Casanova and Eisenstadt[22].

To be post-secular, according to Casanova, does not necessarily mean becoming religious again, but it does mean no longer being convinced that one can become a rational subject only through emancipation from religion.[23] This clearly shows that the criteria for secularisation and modernisation are unclear and thus the assertion of an incompatibility between modernity and religion has become questionable. It also shows that proponents of the secularisation thesis work with a reductionist concept of religion that does not adequately consider non-institutional forms of religion, the so-called covert forms, and that it assumes a gap between pre-modernity and modernity that did not exist.

However, these observations ultimately only point us to the task that secularisation as a major transformation movement draws our attention to, the problem of a definition of religion and the endeavour to conceive religion in its various relationships to society as a whole. Not the abolition of religion, as this is not possible, but rather the need to recognise the transformations of religion in the course of the upheavals of the Enlightenment and modernity is at stake. And this impact is enormous. Secularisation has created a situation of upheaval that is reshaping no less than our assumptions about access to reality, which include the existential questions and attempts at understanding that determine humanity. Those attempts are valid and not lost in this upheaval. Rather, embracing those attempts means recognising religion, or rather religions and religious phenomena themselves, as a critical-transformative undertaking by reflecting on and understanding the relationships in which life stands.

So, there is no doubt, secular does not mean anti-religious, rather secularisation has to be understood as a process in which the dominance of social homogeneity is replaced by subjectivation and pluralisation. This is not a problem for everyone and every religion equally, but it is a particular problem for monotheistic religions, which are based on ideas of unity and derive their systematisation from this. They are, in recognising subjectivation and pluralisation, put under great pressure to transform. However, if this transformation is successful, then tolerance-sensitive encounters with other religions and cultures can be supported and channeled. The decisive factor here is that subjectivation does not become the arbitrariness of isolated individuals, but that the claims to validity that are to be

---

22 See annotations 12 and 14.
23 Cf. José Casanova, "Rethinking Secularization. A Global Comparative Perspective," *The Hedgehog Review* 8 (2006): 7–22.

communicated are retained within them, which enable the question of the shape and meaning of life.

A post-secular rehabilitation of both religion and a non-aporetical secularization can be contributed to by the anthropological turn of religion as a paradigm shift, which allows religion to become an inescapable anthropological datum, as Friedrich Daniel Ernst Schleiermacher accomplished as a friendly transformation to subjectivity and pluralism.

2 The Anthropological Turn of Religion as a Paradigm Shift - On the Transformation of Religion in Modernity using Schleiermacher as an Example

It was F.D.E. Schleiermacher who fundamentally incorporated the transformation of an anthropological turn into his program for defining religion. According to him, the religious henceforth manifests itself not in the idea of God, but in the transcendence of existence. In his reflections on the theory of religion, he endeavors to empirically track down this area of the religious precisely in its function for thought and action and to develop it in terms of the theory of validity. The possibility of doing this stems from his realisation of religious consciousness as that which orients all thought and action.[24] As such, it must be respected and taken into account.

In a discussion with Kant, Schleiermacher makes it clear that it is not possible to reflect on pure reason, on knowledge without presuppositions. This is because knowledge is always embedded in social, historical and cultural conditions. It is therefore not only the path via a 'need of reason', a 'respect for the moral law', as in Kant[25] that brings the transcendent into play, but rather the religious feeling in

---

24 Cf. Friedrich Daniel Ernst Schleiermacher, *Speeches on Religion*, ed. Richard Crouter (Cambridge: Cambridge University Press 2014).

25 Cf. Immanuel Kant, "Grundlegung zur Metaphysik der Sitten," in *Schriften zur Ethik und Religionsphilosophie*, vol. 4, *Immanuel Kant. Werke in sechs Bänden*, ed. Wilhelm Weischedel (Darmstadt: Wissenschaftliche Buchgesellschaft Darmstadt, 1956), 13–14.

the individual that always accompanies thought and action[26]. At the same time, this refers to the experience of the residue of a reason and a vision of a whole, which provides orientation. These experiences – thus determined in the religious feeling of the individual – are not to be confused with observable empiricism. They have categorical status and are nevertheless experienced.

It is precisely this categoriality that is made possible by the particular formation of the individual that Schleiermacher holds in relation to modern subjectivity, and which is intended to reveal the aporetic nature of critical thinking with regard to the understanding of reason. Its achievement is not exhausted in rationality, but in a specific perceptual capacity of paying attention to the whence of being addressed and the whither of responding for which the individual stands, which itself has an inherent responsiveness that is designed for listening and communication. This responsiveness is inaugurated by a passivity that is always already inherent in the individual, i.e. a withdrawal that nevertheless makes itself felt through communication, through responsiveness and resonance, so to speak, and determines the individual.

In contrast to Kant's addressing of the modern subjectivity of reflection, we thus encounter Schleiermacher's focus on the individual[27]. The immediate impressions of such experiences of validity and certainty, which are not accessible to the observable empiricism of a generally verifiable third-person perspective, are evoked in the individual. The distinction between the concept of experience and the special significance of the individual is decisive here. Such experiences transcend the empirical: firstly, in that they – while not conclusive – also do not aim at a whole qua idea or postulate, but can be traced back to a ground that is presupposed as such, and secondly through the effects of contingent encounters that evoke those moods that affect the individual. According to Schleiermacher's insight into the anthropological function of religion, one can or must assume that these effects indicate precisely the obligatory character of religion, which assures individual existence of the certainty of its epistemic reality and moral normativity.

To use the terminology of recent sociology, one could demonstrate this figure. What has recently been demonstrated by the sociologist Hartmut Rosa as the

---

26 Cf. Friedrich Daniel Ernst Schleiermacher, *Der christliche Glaube nach den Grundsätzen der evangelischen Kirche im Zusammenhange dargestellt. Zweite Auflage (1830/31)*, vol. XIII/1, ed. Rolf Schäfer, *Kritische Gesamtausgabe*, (Berlin: De Gruyter, 2003), §4, 32–40.

27 Cf. Friedrich Daniel Ernst Schleiermacher, *Monologen* (Hamburg: Meiner Verlag, 1978).

phenomenon of responsivity and resonance[28] already appears in the constellation of Schleiermacher's theory of religion. The conception of the individual in its form of receptivity, which is expressed with the feeling of ultimate dependence, can claim the concept of resonance for this religious feeling in its effect and the concept of responsiveness for the character of obligation and commitment.

In these aspects of the independence and reflexive grasp of knowledge and action through an intangible ground that runs along with the moods of experience, the reflection-expanding moments that characterise Schleiermacher's concept of religion in the course of the anthropological turn, a paradigm shift is manifested.

It lies in the analysis of the consciousness of transcendence – that characterises the anthropological turn in religion – which no longer expresses itself in reference to God, but in reference to the consciousness of transcendence. This is the reason why, for Schleiermacher, even a religion without God can sometimes be better than one with God.[29] In any case, the position of religion is misjudged if it is identified with either knowledge or morality, but also if knowledge and morality are thought to be independent of religious consciousness. This rules out the possibility of subsuming religion under knowledge and morality in the sense of traditional metaphysics.[30] Such a metaphysics is also outdated, according to Schleiermacher, and can be regarded as superstitious, and such a morality that corresponds to it rightly falls prey to the judgement of either simple uncritical conformism or rigorous fanaticism.

This validation of religion leads Schleiermacher to a clarification of Kant's epistemological concerns, for example with regard to the concept of the transcendental. By adopting this fundamental epistemological concept from Kant, Schleiermacher certainly shares Kant's basic epistemological orientation. This states that the preconditions of cognition are not only to be found in empirical, social and historical conditions, but that these are also subject to categorical preconditions. But Schleiermacher takes this approach further. He does so by referring even more fundamentally to the presuppositional conditions of these transcen-

---

28 Cf. Hartmut Rosa's discovery of Resonance und Responsivity in: Hartmut Rosa, *Resonanz. Eine Soziologie der Weltbeziehung* (Berlin: Suhrkamp Verlag, 2017).

29 Cf. Friedrich Daniel Ernst Schleiermacher, "Über die Religion, Reden an die Gebildeten unter ihren Verächtern (1799)," in *Schriften aus der Berliner Zeit 1769–1799*, vol. I/2, ed. Günter Meckenstock, *Kritische Gesamtausgabe*, (Berlin: De Gruyter, 1984), 185–326.

30 Cf. Friedrich Daniel Ernst Schleiermacher, "Über die Religion, Reden an die Gebildeten unter ihren Verächtern (1799)," in *Schriften aus der Berliner Zeit 1769–1799*, vol. I/2, ed. Günter Meckenstock, *Kritische Gesamtausgabe*, (Berlin: De Gruyter, 1984), 2. Rede, 206–224

dental determinations of thought, which Kant described as a priori. He sees these themselves – contradictorily, as it were – as being bound to experience, but not to experience in the sense of verifiable empiricism, but rather to contingent, unavailable, (intangible) experience in the individual, as can be discovered in feeling through the 'whence' of the so-called "ultimate dependence"[31] and which renders Schleiermacher's individual into the position of a singularity in a qualitative sense. Schleiermacher achieves this with the aforementioned position of the individual, which already points to the possible diversity of religious phenomena.

3 Religion in the Diversity of its Forms – On the Hermeneutical Function of the Concept of Religion

From a categorical point of view, the definition of religion in the course of the paradigm shift of modernity must essentially distinguish between two spheres, which, previously inseparable, have diverged since modern times: the metaphysical, i.e. the theoretical, and the anthropological, which includes the sociological and biological dimension. Subsequently however, it is precisely this existence of both spheres, the criticism and affirmation of religion that also makes it possible to differentiate between religion and the field of the religious, which can also include hidden forms of religion, even those that distance themselves from religion or that define religion in an atheistic way.

Therefore, the paradigm shift of the anthropological turn in religion is characterised by the fact that a broader concept of religion, which encompasses various forms of expression, is becoming dominant. Such forms have sometimes emancipated themselves from the explicit religion in the sense of a specific area or as institutional forms and have found their way into other areas. The resulting diversity of religion, even in its hidden forms, must be taken into account and taken seriously when religion as a phenomenon and concept in modernity is under debate. It shows that modernity has not only relegated religion to the private sphere, but that its concerns remain publicly visible and are passed on or further

---

31 Cf. Friedrich Daniel Ernst Schleiermacher, *Der christliche Glaube nach den Grundsätzen der evangelischen Kirche im Zusammenhange dargestellt. Zweite Auflage (1830/31)*, vol. XIII/1, ed. Rolf Schäfer, *Kritische Gesamtausgabe*, (Berlin: De Gruyter, 2003), §4, 32–40.

developed and transformed in other cultural forms such as, e.g., economics, politics or science. However, this initially gives rise to additional difficulties in the perception and definition of religion, as religion itself becomes diffuse in and with this development and the question of a definition becomes even more problematic. One must reckon with blurring, with transitions, and intermediate phenomena of the term.

In terms of religious studies, the so-called invisible or vagrant religiosity already defined by Thomas Luckmann[32] should be considered here, which, in the course of the differentiation of society, also manifests itself in the aforementioned other social functional areas, in a multifaceted and diverse way. Above all, it is not so easily recognizable. A clarification of the relevance of religion in the modern age must take this multifaceted nature into account, which requires some religious scholars to renounce a positive definition of religion. However, if we now take a look at the existing socio-philosophical conceptual definitions of religion, for example as "overcoming contingency"[33], as an "intention to provide an ultimate justification"[34], as a "competence to differentiate"[35] or as "a transcendence of the self and the world"[36], it immediately becomes clear that this diversity is already in view in order to roughly grasp the phenomenon. For it is only through such perceptions of the diversity and vagueness of the phenomena that it becomes clear that religion is conceived in its conciseness precisely when it includes the potential for distance and difference, even in relation to itself, which in the course of its transformation allows its actual social potential to become clear and unfold. According to Ferdinand Sutterlüthy, it is one of the instances of reflection that characterise modernity, just as art, science and law are.[37]

This is relevant for our investigation in that it becomes clear that it is not arbitrary whether one is aware of the connection between such concealed forms or

---

32 Cf. Thomas Luckmann, *Die unsichtbare Religion* (Berlin: Suhrkamp Verlag, [1991] 2023).

33 Cf. Hermann Lübbe, *Religion nach der Aufklärung* (Graz/Wien/Köln: Styria 1986).

34 Cf. Thomas M. Schmidt, "Absolutheit und Unbedingtheit, idealistische und pragmatistische Strategien der Gottesrede," *Philosophisches Handbuch* 117 (2010/2): 339–350.

35 Cf. Eberhard Jüngel, "Der Gott entsprechende Mensch. Bemerkungen zur Gottebenbildlichkeit des Menschen als Grundfigur theologischer Anthropologie," in *Entsprechungen. Gott – Wahrheit – Mensch*, vol. 2, *Theologische Erörterungen* (Tübingen: Mohr Siebeck, 2002): 290–317; Cf. Elisabeth Gräb-Schmidt, "Die Bedeutung reformatorischer Einsichten für die ethische Urteilsbildung der Gegenwart," in *ZThK* 107 (2010/4): 479–504.

36 Cf. Paul Tillich, *Vorlesungen über Geschichtsphilosophie und Sozialpädagogik (1929/1930)*, vol. 2, ed. Erdmann Sturm, *Gesammelte Werke* (Berlin: De Gruyter 2007).

37 Cf. Ferdinand Suterlüthy, see annotation 17.

The Anthropological Turn of Religion — **57**

of the complexity of what religion stands for or not. In any case, the anthropological turn in religion makes it clear that humans are not satisfied with the mere immanence of the here and now. Knut Wenzel, a Catholic theologian from the University of Frankfurt, emphasizes - as Schleiermacher already had[38] - that this longing does not have to be theistically linked to a personal God. For it is precisely in its various forms of expression that religion can point to its relevance today.[39] According to Thomas Schmidt, Religion is the system that 'represents in its purity the immanence - transcendence - difference that is operationally at work everywhere'.[40]

With this diversity and concealment of the forms of the religious, an expansion of the complexity of the religious itself becomes apparent; the former concept of religious theory now is liquefied into the narrative, which depicts different perspectives and enables plural forms. However, it is precisely these plural forms that are decisive for modernity, which can no longer assume a general holistic view. The old question of being is thus not dispensed with, but it is stripped of a visible object-hood as well as a blind fundamental dimension and finds in the perspective of anthropological self-understanding an existential proof of reality in its interpretative and experiencing process character, appropriate to human access. As such, it can take account of the plurality of the modern age without dissolving it into arbitrariness and, with this, saying goodbye to the question of validity and normativity that religion is also about. This hermeneutical quality of religious awareness – in the sense of awareness of difference – thus presupposes a self-relativisation of concrete forms of expression of religion from within itself, without having to jeopardise the persuasive power of the religious, which is based on the experience of an event in its capacity of disclosure: its so-called resonance, and without underestimating the concrete forms of expression to which the disclosure remains bound which obtains responsive support. Such a hermeneutics of resonance and responsiveness is fundamentally orientated towards difference, namely for the purpose of understanding pluriform identities. Religion can thus also take on hermeneutical tasks in the religious practice of self-understanding in an interreligious and intercultural dialogue.

---

38 Friedrich Daniel Ernst Schleiermacher, "Über die Religion, Reden an die Gebildeten unter ihren Verächtern (1799)," in *Schriften aus der Berliner Zeit 1769 -1799*, vol. I/2, ed. Günter Meckenstock, *Kritische Gesamtausgabe*, (Berlin: De Gruyter, 1984), 245.

39 This is not only the case in the realm of the sacred, but also in the domain of art. Cf. Knut Wenzel, *Die Wucht des Undarstellbaren* (Freiburg: Herder Verlag, 2019).

40 Thomas M. Schmidt in Rolf Wiggershaus (own translation), see annotation 17, 12.

In this way, the hermeneutical orientation of religion in the modern age refers not only to tolerance, but also to an openness to others.

Religion, therefore, is indispensable for hermeneutical thinking in the diversity of global religious cultures, which faces up to the comprehension of reality within the framework of our finite perspective and the broken fragility of human-historical existence.

4 Religion as a Placeholder for the Metaphysical Void in Modernity - On the Normative Dimension of the Concept of Religion

To summarise:

The resulting diversity of the religious, even in its concealed forms, must be taken into account and taken seriously. It is important that the concept of religion as a concept emerges at a time in which it should also fulfil a placeholder function, namely to be a placeholder for the lost metaphysical ground and ontological self-understanding.

In any case, the path to modernity cannot be travelled by saying goodbye to religion, nor by repressing it into the private sphere in the sense of rigorous religious isolation and then also fundamentalist, intolerant self-assertion. Rather, religion must be included in the project of modernity. However, cultural anthropological and sociological descriptions of religion are not enough to do justice to the phenomenon of religion. Only when these phenomena can actually be embedded not only in empirical (on the one hand) and speculative (on the other), but also in practically demonstrable procedures, the modern claim of religion is satisfied, which now transports the formerly metaphysical dimension by reaching out to transcendence.

This reference to transcendence therefore remains of fundamental importance. For without it, we lose our claim to reality and, with regard to the question of meaning, we remain stuck with individualistic questions of taste or subjectivist declarations of certainty. Perhaps a post-traditional society could live well with this. However, this would not do justice to the theoretical standards of modern religious research, nor would it do justice to the actual weight of religion for thinking, on the one hand, and for the conduct of life, on the other, as Schleiermacher earlier emphasised. This weight depends on the reality-guaranteeing experiences of the individual, which make it possible to reach out to the transcendent-transcendental, which – as has been shown – can make itself felt in various areas.

The paradigm shift, which means the abandonment of traditional metaphysics of substance or ontology and which results in the anthropological turn, which Jürgen Habermas, for example, has labelled a post-metaphysical age[41], such a paradigm shift does not abolish religion, but it also commits religion to a new sobriety, without however abandoning its yearning heart. This is where the reference to transcendence comes into play, by which religion can be defined in modernity, and which represents the reminiscence of former metaphysical concerns.

And just as it was already visible in what Karl Jaspers called the Axis period 2 ½ thousand years ago[42], and which now also claims validity after secularisation, such a paradigm shift can also overcome the Eurocentric view of a rational narrowing of secularisation, in that both, religion as a concept and religion in its plural forms of different religions, can be grasped with it. According to Hermann Deuser, this reference to transcendence still means the facilitation of distancing criticism of very different fields of application[43] which, even according to Habermas, in its recognition and reformulation in the Enlightenment period signifies a "revolution in the way of thinking, which can rightly be described as such in terms of the history of religion."[44] If this is true, then "the concept of transcendence is particularly characteristic of an innovation that is still in force today."[45] According to Hans Joas, this innovation includes "criticism, reflexivity, moral universalism and insight into the symbolic nature of symbols"[46], to which Habermas adds a "growing awareness of contingency"[47].

In this way, religion can certainly be linked to the paradigm shift of secularisation in the history of mentalities and be installed in parallel. However, this presupposes a secularisation that is aware of the multi-layered nature of its concept, which therefore encompasses not only the critical line of religion, but also the

---

41 Cf. Jürgen Habermas, "Glaube und Wissen. Friedenspreisrede 2001," in *Zeitdiagnosen. Zwölf Essays*, ed. Jürgen Habermas (Frankfurt a.M.: Suhrkamp Verlag, 2003): 249–262.

42 Karl Jaspers, *Vom Ursprung und Ziel der Geschichte* (München: R. Piper, [1949] 1963).

43 Cf. Hermann Deuser, "Säkularisierung und Sakrament," in *Religion realistisch*, ed. Hermann Deuser (Tübingen: Mohr Siebeck, 2023): 43–69, see especially 46.

44 Jürgen Habermas, *Die okzidentale Konstellation von Glauben und Wissen*, vol. 1 of *Auch eine Geschichte der Philosophie* (Frankfurt a.M.: Suhrkamp Verlag, 2019), 186.

45 Hermann Deuser, "Säkularisierung und Sakrament," in *Religion realistisch*, ed. Hermann Deuser (Tübingen: Mohr Siebeck, 2023): 43–69, 45.

46 Cf. Hans Joas, *Die Macht des Heiligen. Eine Alternative zur Geschichte von der Entzauberung* (Berlin: Suhrkamp 2017), 444f. (as cited in Deuser, see Annotation 60, 45.)

47 Jürgen Habermas, *Vernünftige Freiheit. Spuren des Diskurses über Glauben und Wissen*, vol. 2 of *Auch eine Geschichte der Philosophie* (Frankfurt a.M.: Suhrkamp Verlag, 2019), 188.

affirmative line of theory of religion, and secures its lasting right. Then, with the anthropological turn of religion, it remains to be noted that in all endeavors towards autonomy, religion should be understood as transcendental consciousness and that this is in no way opposed to autonomy. This fundamental connection between religion or transcendence and reason is obscured by the proponents of the secularisation thesis, but also - and no less - by the unreflective references to a 'return of religion'[48] with which any criticism of religion is to be banished.

Accordingly, it is important to bring into play the differential function of religion that lies in the reference to transcendence. In fact, it is the argument that prevents religion from both, claiming a pious special area and potentially instrumentalising it, and leaving the field to those esoterics or zealots who are currently increasingly discrediting religion again. After all, *homo religiosus* is not labelled as such because he or she does not want to represent his or her maturity and freedom, but because he or she needs religion or the reference to transcendence in the diversity of its forms, including its concealed forms, for emancipation and freedom. Understanding this connection is the task of serious philosophical research into religion – as was initiated by Schleiermacher and as we are called upon to do again today.

Neither the thesis of disappearance nor the invocations of return do justice to the anthropological phenomenon of the religious in its transcendental function for thought and action – indeed for human existence as such – but those figures that encompass phenomena of the religious in the broadest sense, which – possibly also at a distance from religion – incorporate an awareness of transcendence into one's own operations of thought and action, and thus recognise the legacy of religion in the modern age – the *fait religieux*[49] according to Delumeau – also and especially under the guise of secularity.

Accordingly, modern religion rightly defends itself against a pre-critical re-ontologisation, but not against the claim to visualise reality and normativity. This can be and is still present, but now in the guise of practical processes of realisation and interpretation that become visible on the anthropological level.

The concept of religion as a reference to transcendence stands for the fact that freedom and emancipation do not regress into alienation and heteronomy, even

---

48 Cf. Martin Riesebrodt, *Die Rückkehr der Religionen* (München: C.H. Beck, 2000); Martin Riesebrodt, *Cultus und Heilsversprechen. Eine Theorie der Religionen.* (München: C.H. Beck, 2007).

49 Jean Delumeau, *Le Fait religieux* (Paris: Fayard, 1993).; Cf. Elisabeth Gräb-Schmidt, Benjamin Häfele, Christian P. Hölzchen, eds., *Rationalität und Transzendenz, MthSt* 132 (Leipzig: Evangelische Verlagsanstalt Leipzig, 2019).

after the significant turning point of the European "saddle time". Remaining aware of its symbolic significance as an anchor for emancipation and freedom, for self-assurance and self-determination as well as for the ability to be pluralistic, is the task of a modern understanding of religion, which cannot see religion as a loss, but rather as a gain of self-understanding and an offer of orientation for an open society.

Vincent Goossaert

Gods as persons and subjects: Proposals from China for a comparative approach

My work[1] over the last thirty years or so has led me to spend time with the Chinese gods.[2] The historical context in which this essay is grounded is the modern Chinese world, from the sixteenth century onwards. I have gradually come to realize that, despite a fairly rich historiography on certain gods in particular, very little theoretical or analytical work has focused on how they exist and interact with humans. While much work focuses on cults, i.e. social representations and practices, and thus on the ways humans appropriate the gods to satisfy their own needs and affirm their values and aspirations, very few scholars ask the question of what these gods are and what they do. Yet Chinese data are particularly rich and have much to contribute to the field of religious studies on this question of the forms of existence and action of the gods. An impressive number of Chinese gods are clearly defined persons with whom humans have interpersonal relations; some of them even behave like subjects, speaking of themselves from the interiority of their divine person (that is, a god endowed with a unique persona) and acting in ways that surprise their human interlocutors. Indeed, my more recent work on Chinese spirit-writing caused me to explore vast amounts of revealed texts where gods speak in the first person, about themselves and their relations to humans and other gods. My question is: what enables or limits this emergence of divine persons and subjects in China and elsewhere? Here, I propose to develop an analytical framework that can account for historical and ethnographic data from China and other cultural contexts.

Taking the gods seriously as persons and, even more so, as subjects, implies recognizing their agency and therefore their existence, which remains a stum-

---

1 I am deeply indebted to many colleagues and friends with whom we exchanged views on these issues and who helped me with their critical remarks and reading advice; in particular Isabelle Charleux, Grégory Delaplace, Theodora Jim, Yang Qin, Benoit Fliche, Christophe Pons, Marcus Bingenheimer, Matthias Hayek, and Bernard Faure. This work was developed as part of the "Divine Saving in Greek and Chinese Polytheism" project, directed by Theodora Jim (Nottingham University) and funded by the Leverhulme Trust, 2022–2025.
2 I mean "god" here in a very broad sense; we will see in the definitions that follow that it is a type of invisible being capable of changing human destiny.

∂ Open Access. © 2025 the author(s), published by De Gruyter. (cc) BY This work is licensed under the Creative Commons Attribution 4.0 International License.
https://doi.org/10.1515/9783112218907-005

bling block in humanities and social sciences. My personal position on gods is agnostic, which in no way prevents me from observing that a model in which gods, spirits, and other invisible entities exist is clearly an efficient and rational way of accounting for the data, since these entities have effects that cannot easily be explained otherwise. I develop such a model without making any assumptions as to their mode of existence. I am particularly interested in the ritual devices that enable such effects to be created by invisible entities, and thus the emergence of divine persons and subjects. These devices create reciprocal relationships between different kinds of entities, including humans and others, all of which must be taken seriously as part of these relationships.

Before describing the model, I need to briefly clarify what this essay is not about. First of all, belief. I am not denying the existence or relevance of belief, but it seems to me that it is as much a consequence as a cause of the relationships between humans and invisible entities enabled by ritual devices.[3] Second, cognitivist approaches are also highly relevant (for example, they elucidate the conditions under which a human recognizes the agency of other entities), but limit the analysis to humans, which is not my aim here, since I am seeking to apprehend the emergence of non-human persons and subjects. Third, anthropological theories belonging to the ontological turn have also inspired me, but I wish to keep them at a distance here. Ontologies do indeed define different ways of attributing agency and personality among entities, which overlaps with my concerns. However, I am more interested than ontological theories are (or, as I understand them to be) in the processes of change of ontological state affecting all entities, processes that are at work in every culture. Rather than identifying cultures in which spirits are, or are not, persons, do or do not have an interiority, I prefer to explore across cultures processes through which invisibles acquire or loose a persona or an interiority.

This essay begins with a very schematic set of definitions, which, despite their abstract and generalizing nature, seem to me to be necessary in a comparative framework if we are to know precisely what we are talking about when we evoke "persons," "subjects," "invisibles," etc. across different cultures. For this, we need

---

3 Andrea De Antoni, "Steps to an Ecology of Spirits. Comparing Feelings of More-than-Human, Immaterial Meshworks?," *More-than-Human Worlds: A NatureCulture Blog Series*, https://www.natcult.net/steps-to-an-ecology-of-spirits/. Tanya M. Luhrmann, *How God Becomes Real: Kindling the Presence of Invisible Others* (Princeton: Princeton University Press, 2020), envisages belief as a worldview permanently transformed and shaped by practices of familiarization with invisible entities.

to let go of our deeply ingrained concepts of person and subject in order to build them anew as comparative concepts.

This set of definitions does not aim to classify entities and cultures, but to help us think through processes of transformation. Having a system of definition does not prevent us from suspending qualification for as long as possible in each case studied, as anthropologists recommend, since in the analytical framework proposed here, entities often move from one category to another within the field of possibilities marked out by definitions. In the second part, I will discuss the types of ritual devices through or in which entities can acquire (or lose) the status of person or subject, and then the political or ideological constraints that limit the use of such devices – since it is rarely taken for granted that invisible entities that tend to assert themselves as persons or subjects should be left free to do as they wish. Third, I will sketch out some comparative questions from China to a few privileged comparenda, especially ancient Greece.

1 Definitions

The definitions proposed here are based on the perspective (perceptive capacities) of a living human. They do not claim to describe what exists in a general way, still less to define an ontology, but simply to provide a useful mode of analysis of the observable relationships of humans with other entities. They are pragmatic, and often at odds with common definitions in the immense literature in philosophy, psychology, psychoanalysis, and anthropology, among other fields, on the notions of entity and agent on the one hand, and person and subject on the other.

1.1 Modes of existence

I am interested here in entities (or beings), defined as material and/or symbolic configurations perceptible by a human, whether through the physical and/or mental senses. All entities tend to perpetuate themselves, that is, continue to exist and/or replicate or reproduce.

The present system of definition leaves aside the question of reality, and does not distinguish between "real" and "non-real" entities. I propose instead there are many modes of existence; some well-known and described (such as biological life or physical objects), others only supposed and theoretical (including, here, the invisibles and in particular the gods), others still unknown; the number of modes of existence is open, possibly unlimited.[4] Thus, I do justice to Albert Piette or Tanya Luhrmann, who insist that the relationship between human and god is not a relationship between equals. On the other hand, I do not conclude from this, as Luhrmann, Piette, and other scholars do, that gods do not exist and that we must therefore make an effort to believe in them in spite of everything.[5] There is no reason to exclude from the analysis entities that belong to a mode of existence that is hypothesized but not objectively observed – just as scholars of physics integrate into their theoretical models particles or other elements that are assumed but not yet observed and nonetheless account well for observed data. The usefulness of the analytical model proposed here will be judged by its ability to account for observed data in a simpler and more convincing way than other models—such as conceptualizing gods as collective representations, or narratives, or cultural schemas (memes)—, and not by its a priori validity.

A non-exhaustive list of modes of existence relevant to our needs includes the following seven:

a) biological life: humans, animals, plants;
b) physical objects;
c) machines: physical and/or symbolic devices that produce (in a predictable and stable way) a result when given inputs, such as computers or AIs;
d) symbols or memes: images, texts, ideas, which can be reproduced using, among others, entities having biological life (carrying them from mind to mind), but also machines (for example, self-replicating viruses) as material supports or relays[6];
e) institutions: a stable network of entities of various natures whose interactions produce a coherent result. Institutions are agents, and can be persons (legal persons). For example: the state, companies, a church, the academic world…;
f) invisibles: entities which are not always (usually not) perceptible to humans, perception depending on certain circumstances, or devices set up for the pur-

---

4 Étienne Souriau, *Les différents modes d'existence: Suivi de "Du mode d'existence de l'œuvre à faire"*. Présentation par Isabelle Stengers et Bruno Latour (Paris: Puf, 2015).

5 Albert Piette, "L'entité jusqu'au bout. À propos de la question ontologique en anthropologie," *Religiologiques: sciences humaines et religion* 43 (2022): 91–111; Luhrmann, *How God Becomes Real*.

6 Richard Dawkins, *The Selfish Gene* (Oxford: Oxford University Press, 1976).

pose, but also partly on something other than the will or abilities of humans.[7] Invisibles can have the quality of persons (metapersons, or spirits and gods) and even subjects. The fact that we know nothing (the author of these lines, at any rate) about the substratum and functioning of this mode of existence, unlike the previous five, in no way prevents us from describing its effects;

g) nothingness: entities inaccessible to other entities other than through speculation.

1.2 Degree of singularity

In several modes of existence, each entity can evolve on a scale from the least to the most singular in its relationship to other entities, from a poorly identified entity, perceived by a highly indeterminate, generic form of relationship, to a subject that constantly reminds others of its irreducible singularity (or uniqueness). To dispel any ambiguity, I hasten to add that by singularity I do not mean separation from other entities; to the contrary, I propose that singularity is built through relations to other entities. Also, singular here is not the opposite of plural but of indeterminate: a highly singular entity can at the same time be plural (having several personas).

Naturally, entities existing as physical objects or machines cannot become persons and even less subjects; but biological living beings, invisibles, and some others can. This scale is undoubtedly in reality a gradient of infinite possibilities, but for the purposes of comparative analysis, I propose five degrees (or states), none of which is permanent.[8] The following five definitions are a chain of nesting: each state or degree is a sub-category of the previous one:

---

7 Grégory Delaplace, "Introduction. L'invisible tel qu'il apparaît," *Ateliers d'anthropologie* 52 (2022).

8 I was tempted to call them "ontological status," but this term is too suggestive of stability, hence my preference for degree or state.

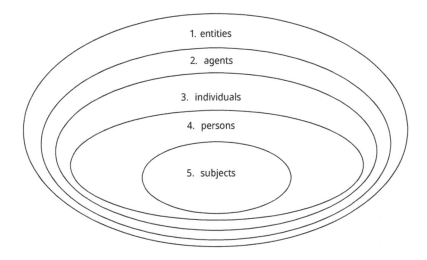

1. *Entity*: a material and/or symbolic configuration perceptible to a human being, whether through the physical and/or mental senses, as defined above.

2. *Agent*: an entity that can interact with and have an effect on other entities. The interactions envisaged here depend on human observation, but can take place on different levels: ordinary physical life, mental experiences (dreams, visualizations), representations (literature, theater, ritual...). The process by which an entity moves to degree 2 is **agentification**.

A crucial assumption of my analytical model is that every interaction potentially has lasting consequences, including on other levels. For instance, a god talking to another god on stage in a play creates an interaction between them that (potentially) has consequences in entirely other contexts (e.g., in devotees' dreams, in worship practice, etc.), including by people who have not seen the play in question.

The notion of agent is of course inspired by Bruno Latour's work and Actor-network theory, but I depart from it here insofar as Latour considers agents as (a priori) without interiority, whereas I am particularly interested in the way in which, as agents and through their relations, some entities can become a person and even a subject, i.e. acquire interiority (having previously or simultaneously acquired individuality, which constitutes the next degree).

3. *Individual*: an agent recognized as unique and stably identifiable through a name, an appearance, or a way of acting—I add that a unique individual agent can be a plurality, as is quite common in ancient Greek religion but is likely found in most polytheist traditions: a group of gods acting together and recognized as such under a common name is an individual entity. This definition of individual is

clearly distinct from the modern commonsense use of "individual." The process by which an agent moves to degree 3 is **individuation**. To take an example among invisibles, exorcism often implies individuation: the agent causing harm is first identified (by a human, or asked to itself decline its identity) and then dealt with nominally – Chinese exorcisms are typically judicial processes beginning with summoning and asserting identities.

Many individuals are not persons, for example, certain animals that are not recognized as having consciousness, or, in the mode of existence of the invisible, the force of a natural site (a stone, a spring, a river...); or even a meme. If we consider that the gods are memes (symbols invented by humans, which are transmitted through representations and stories), then they are not persons. But then they do not have some of the properties that persons have in the invisible mode of existence (notably, consciousness and the ability to subjectivize).

In the Chinese context, as in others, many invisible individuals have a title but no proper name: the earth god of a particular settlement, of a particular mountain, of rain or wind... Many are designated by their function, like the indispensable but anonymous little hands of the celestial bureaucracy – such as the innumerable *gongcao* 功曹, "officers of merit," who process divine paperwork, some being assigned to a particular time of day or a particular area of space. This does not prevent some of them from occasionally seeking to become persons. An invisible individual (an individually identified spirit or god) does not need to become a person in order to do what is expected of it as a god, i.e. answer prayers. But, in certain circumstances, the relationships humans form with this invisible individual enable it to emerge as a person. One of the reasons for this is that an important part of the way humans "do" religion is not purely utilitarian (we do not pray just to obtain concrete benefits), but is based on the intrinsic value some humans place on the interpersonal relationship they form with invisible entities: this essential point has been highlighted by Tanya Luhrmann.[9]

4. *Person*: an individual whom other individuals credit with a conscience, i.e. who knows itself and is responsible for its actions. The process by which an individual moves to degree 4 is **personification**. Its opposite, de-personification, merges or confuses that person with other persons, into an individual or even a simple generic agent, still active but without its own specific conscience and story.[10]

---

9 Luhrmann, *How God Becomes Real*.
10 Susan Naquin, *Gods of Mount Tai: Familiarity and the Material Culture of North China, 1000-2000* (Leiden: Brill, 2022), argues (but based on visual evidence only) that this is what happened

As the person knows, and other persons also know, its actions, it has a history, and therefore potentially a biography (but autobiography, on the other hand, requires a subject to be enunciated). A person is an entity that other persons relate to in the context of their interpersonal relationships, not as abstract providers of benefits or information but as persons knowing (to some extent) each other's history, and the history of their own relations. The person is therefore fundamentally social, constituted in its relationship with others. I therefore define "personal god," a term widely used in religious studies but defined differently by different authors, as a god with whom humans enter into person-to-person relationships – we will see that in some cases, these relationships can become intersubjective.

For some scholars, in some contexts at least, the person is just that: a sum of discrete relationships and the stories linked to those relationships, a "dividual" formed from a sum. For example, Barend ter Haar has analyzed the god Guandi 關帝 as the sum of stories told about him by distinct groups.[11] Such an analysis is consistent with my model if the person in question does not subjectivize – which is not the case with Guandi. Furthermore, a relational approach (to define a person by its relationships) does not per se preclude a coherence of that person. In my own work on the social networks of gods in spirit-writing contexts, I found that those with the most numerous and intense relationships with other gods had the most coherent, well-defined personalities, precisely because all these interactions provided them with opportunities to reaffirm and develop their personality, rather than atomizing it in distinct, dyadic facets.[12]

Persons exist in various modes of existence, including humans and animals, as well as the invisible (the metaperson defined by Marshall Sahlins as the everyday partners of the vast majority of humans in everyday interpersonal relationships).[13] At present (2025), AIs are only machines (they have no observable consciousness); however, in the projects of many developers, and in the representations found notably in science fiction, AIs have acquired consciousness and thus become persons; there is therefore reason to consider them potentially as persons.

---

in modern (seventeenth-twentieth centuries) times to the major north China goddess Bixia yuanjun 碧霞元君.

11 Barend Ter Haar, *Guan Yu: the Religious Afterlife of a Failed Hero* (Oxford: Oxford University Press, 2017).

12 Vincent Goossaert, "The Social Networks of Gods in Late Imperial Spirit-writing Altars," *Religions* 14.2, 217 (2023), https://doi.org/10.3390/rel14020217.

13 Marshall Sahlins, "Cosmic Economics," *Annals of the Fondazione Luigi Einaudi* 55 (2021): 255–78.

A person is defined by one or more **persona** (or personality): a stable, coherent set of values, motivations and abilities expressed socially by a person; its "specifications."[14] A person has at least one persona (more or less rich, complex, thick) and can have several personas: this is, I readily admit, a heterodox aspect of my model. A human being can have several personas in different social contexts: professional, family, role-playing, etc. In some contexts, a person with excessively different personas is considered pathological, but the limit is fluid.[15] Invisible persons' ability to have different personas is much greater than that of humans (or institutions): their temporality can be much longer, and they can form relationships with a wider variety of entities. This extends to gender identities: invisible persons can more easily have a female persona and a male one than humans. The diversity of personas of invisible persons, notably gods, has been variously expressed (with a specific name or iconography, often linked to a specific place) in various cultures: the avatars of Hindu gods, the epithets of Greek gods, etc. The question of the unity and multiplicity of any given god, which has been the subject of much discussion in various fields (ancient Greece, India, among others), seems to me to be usefully approached in this way: it is in the very nature of invisible persons to be able to be many and yet one by having several personas.

Humans can endow a person (especially an invisible person) with a new persona, for example a pre-existing fictional character who appears in a new light in a new story, or a god about whom new stories are told in which it behaves differently. Cultures have varying degrees of tolerance for dissonance between different personas of the same person, human or otherwise. Frequently, a new persona deemed incompatible with existing ones will be rejected and assigned to a different person: it is then decided that it is not the same person, but another one who was confused with it. In China, the personas of the same god generally seem highly compatible. This is the case, for example, with the different personas of Guanyin 觀音 (the bodhisattva of compassion), arguably the most widespread personal god in the Chinese world, who has different iconographies, names, stories, and behaviors, some of which are linked to previous incarnations or lives, but all of which are considered coherent and emanating from the same person.[16] The case is

---

14 Elisabeth Claverie, *Les guerres de la Vierge. Une anthropologie des apparitions* (Paris: Gallimard, 2003).
15 Christophe Pons, "La possibilité de ne pas être soi. Sujet, spiritisme et libre-arbitre au Portugal," *Journal des anthropologues* 164–165 (2021): 111–29.
16 Yü Chün-fang, *Kuan-yin: the Chinese Transformation of Avalokitesvara* (New York: Columbia University Press, 2001).

comparable with that of the Virgin Mary, who also has different names and personas in different places and icons, but all of these are recognized as belonging to the same person.

The Greek gods, whom Vernant famously describes as powers rather than persons,[17] are here, according to my definitions, persons with multiple personas, and therefore weak coherence. Vernant's central argument is in fact that the Greek gods are not subjects and have no interiority; if we clearly distinguish, as I attempt to do here, person and subject, then we can reformulate Vernant's argument in this way without losing any of its force. Indeed, recent scholarship on Greek religion has reconciled with the idea of various local cult personas autonomous but deeply related to the one god figure known from myth.[18] It is also from this perspective that we can approach the multiple nature of the Hindu gods, and the existence of multiple forms, notably the avatars of Vishnu and Shiva; each of these gods is a person with multiple and very different autonomous personas.[19]

The question of coherence between a person's manifestations and actions, and also between its different personas, is essential to my model. It is first appreciated in an emic way by those who interact with this invisible person. The coherence of an invisible person is linked to the general conception of what is a person in the society in question, and therefore varies according to cultural contexts; it also varies according to a culture's set of notions concerning the invisibles. It is not primarily up to the scholar to decide whether a god is coherent; it is up to the humans who are in relationship with this divine person to react or not when faced with dissonance. The scholar can sometimes be surprised, like Hendrik Versnel for the Greek gods, at the great tolerance humans have for assertions about their gods that seem contradictory to him.[20] Yet, emic reactions to discrepancies in divine personas do exist; when Chinese practitioners of a spirit-writing cult witness statements that seem incompatible with the persona of the god expressing itself, they do not hesitate to cry "impersonation," assuming that some ill-

---

17 Jean-Pierre Vernant, "Aspects de la personne dans la religion grecque," in *Mythe et pensée chez les Grecs, Études de psychologie historique* (Paris: Maspero, 1965).

18 Vinciane Pirenne-Delforge and Gabriella Pironti, "Many vs. One," in *The Oxford Handbook of Ancient Greek Religion*, ed. Esther Eidinow & Julia Kindt (Oxford: Oxford University Press, 2015), 39–47.

19 Marie-Louise Reiniche, "Un nom, une forme, un lieu: L'invention hindoue de l'autre et du même," *Revue de l'histoire des religions* 205.4 (1988): 367–83; Christopher John Fuller, *The Camphor Flame: Popular Hinduism and Society in India* (Princeton: Princeton University Press, 2004), chapter 2, "Gods and Goddesses."

20 Hendrik Simon Versnel, *Coping with the Gods* (Leiden: Brill, 2011).

intentioned little spirit is impersonating the god in question. One of the crucial elements humans use to determine coherence of an invisible is morality; gods are often defined by moral values (or lack of them). What the scholar can do, noting that humans accept the coherence of a god with whom they relate in many different ways (and often in relation to the different functions these gods perform), is to identify the elements of stability, the invariant values and character traits. I had the opportunity to carry out this work concerning a thunder god, Wang lingguan 王靈官, who has been active in China since the twelfth century in a wide variety of contexts: hagiographic narratives, rituals for the salvation of the dead, pilgrimages, sworn oaths, exorcisms, theater, and liturgical initiations.[21]

5. *Subject*: a person who speaks in the first person ("I"), expresses a persona (a person can therefore have several subjects, just as it has several personas), and manifests desires and interiority. This interiority is in part unknowable, even to the person itself: this is the "subjective division" defined by Lacan, who sees the role of the subject as an expression of the unconscious – for the purposes of the present work, however, I am not including the question of the unconscious in the model. The subject emanates from a person, but is not the same as (and may be in a tense relationship with) that person. The self is defined here as the object of the subject's discourse (i.e. one of the person's personas describing itself). It is therefore not a substantial, preexisting substratum of the person, in contrast to what is assumed in mainstream humanities, as well as many (but by not means all) vernacular and religious understandings of the self.

The subject asserts specific intentions and projects, and can surprise its interlocutors. Thus, one can ritually control (or at least reasonably hope to control) an invisible person who is not subjectivized – this person will, quite reliably, do what it is told to do. Chinese examples abound; various kinds of ancestors, sages, and territorial gods, among others, are reputed to enforce divine codes and reward virtue, without taking any personal initiative and expressing individual preferences (*si* 私, widely vilified in Daoist texts on the invisibles). Control over subjects, on the other hand, is imperfect at best: the subject is constantly overflowing, and this is what defines it. The emergence of a subject is always unsettling. Not every person behaves as a subject (not all the time, or ever). The subject is therefore a less stable state than the person.

---

21 Vincent Goossaert, "Ritual Techniques for Creating a Divine Persona in Late Imperial China: The Case of Daoist Law Enforcer Lord Wang," *Journal of Chinese Religions* 50 (2022): 45–76.

We still need to distinguish between two types of subject: **potential and actual**.[22] A character in a play who says "I..." is a subject, but not in the same way as I (Vincent Goossaert writing these lines) am a subject when I say "I" talking to my nearest and dearest. The former is potential: it is a staged subject, but totally constrained by the director; it cannot overflow unless it unexpectedly goes completely off-script (obviously, cases of going off-script are more easily observed in ethnography or modern historical documentation than in ancient history). The second, on the other hand, is controlled only by itself. For all that, the potential subject – the staged god, for example, who speaks for itself – creates the conditions that make it possible for the actual subject to emerge, even if this emergence has to take place in other circumstances. A culture in which we never read, see, or hear a god speaking about itself as a subject will find it much harder to allow divine subjects to emerge, even spontaneously. Conversely, in a culture where we witness this kind of divine first-person speaking in literature, the performing arts, games, and elsewhere, it is unlikely that gods will not somehow emerge as actual subjects, whether through mediums, in dreams, or other means. Drawing the line between potential invisible subjects and real ones is a tricky business. On stage, how much room is there for improvisation, for overflow? And in the written collections of divine utterances (oracles), what editing work has been carried out, sometimes undoubtedly eliminating overflowing utterances? Oracles, as they have come down to us in Greece, Japan or elsewhere, are perhaps just as scripted as plays – but we also find, for example in the new Japanese religions of the nineteenth century, utterly overflowing outbursts.[23]

The process by which a person moves on to degree 5 is **subjectivation**, i.e. the process (notably involving the relational/ritual devices that create its conditions of possibility) of emergence and expression of the subject. Its opposite (deciding to cease, or being made to cease expressing oneself as a subject) is desubjectivation (a god ceasing to appear and talk as a subject). The framework for subjectivation (at least in the definitions I use) is language in the broadest sense, which provides a binding cultural framework (Lacan's "Other," *autre*). This, I admit, is a very

---

22 This distinction between potential and actual has no relevance to other degrees of singularity, including persons.

23 Matthias Hayek has drawn my attention to the overflowing (unexpected, unsettling) divine speech revealed (through possession) in new religions such as Ōmotokyō 大本教 (founded 1892) or Tenrikyō 天理教, compared to the earlier collections of oracles. On contemporary Japanese oracles, see Anne Bouchy, *Les oracles de Shirataka: vie d'une femme spécialiste de la possession dans le Japon du XXe siècle* (Toulouse: Presses Universitaires du Mirail, 2005).

anthropocentric framework. As a result, the possibilities for subjectivation vary widely from one cultural context to another. What is more, and this is the core of my definitional and analytical system, it depends on culturally available relational and ritual possibilities (techniques that are known and mastered, and socially/culturally accepted). For example, in a culture where possession and letting the invisibles speak is commonplace and well-accepted, the possibilities for subjectivation are considerably greater than in cultures that do not practice or disapprove of such techniques.

One of the properties of the subject is the formulation and exchange of affects. We can conceive of affects as pre-existing any persons,[24] but the expression of affects (pleasure, pain, fear, love...) is specific to the subjects who express their feelings to others. The content of intersubjective exchanges between humans and the invisibles typically contains a large proportion of descriptions of affects on both sides, which are either absent or only marginally present (on the god's part at any rate) in formal exchanges addressed to personal but not subjectivized gods. A prayer to a personal god can express human affects, but this is quite different from intersubjective interaction.

The general pattern outlined above can be considered on a number of different scales. On a macro level, many historians of religion will recognize in it the process, well described in numerous examples, of the gradual emergence, sometimes over centuries or even millennia, of "great gods" from "little gods" or even demons or anonymous forces[25] ; these entities acquire a name, a persona and a history, then come to exercise sovereignty by asserting their will as all-powerful subjects. But these phenomena of change of degree are more finely and precisely observed on a micro scale.

A second important point concerns the increasing anthropomorphization of entities as they progress through the stages leading to personhood and then subjecthood. This is undoubtedly linked to the cognitive possibilities and constraints of humans, which make it very difficult, perhaps impossible, for them to maintain interpersonal and, even more so, intersubjective relationships with entities that

---

24 Andrea De Antoni, "Affect," in *The International Encyclopedia of Anthropology*, ed. Hilary Callan (Hoboken: John Wiley & Sons, 2020).

25 For an analysis of this process in terms of subjectivation, based on Chinese examples, see Vincent Goossaert, "Petits dieux chinois," in *Entre évitement et alliance, Formes mineures du divin*, ed. Jean-Pierre Albert and Agnes Kedzierska Manzon (Turnhout: Brepols, 2024, pp. 77–92). On a very different note, I cannot resist mentioning Terry Pratchett's novel *Small Gods* (London: Victor Gollancz, 1992).

bear absolutely no resemblance to them. By anthropomorphization and resemblance here, I refer to behavior, rather than bodily aspect, which is secondary. The gods with whom humans develop this type of relationship are, functionally, like humans, even if – as is often the case in China – they were initially explicitly identified as animals, or even plants or minerals.[26] The urge to humanize certain entities in no way precludes the existence of other, very powerful entities, with whom we maintain non-personal relationships that have major consequences. A disease or an evil force, for example, can be identified as an invisible but very real and frightening individual, one which concerned humans must confront, but which they refuse to consider as a person. Humans do not humanize all invisibles (and other entities), but they do encourage to humanize themselves those they want to let become persons, and even more so subjects – a very particular, and in a sense privileged, corner of the vast world of the invisibles.

2 Mutations

The above system of definitions describes states observed in entities; all of them are subject to change, in both their mode of existence and their degree of singularity.

2.1 Change of mode of existence

An entity may change its mode of existence, either ephemerally or permanently, and may or may not retain some or all of the properties of its previous mode of existence. For example:

* living→invisible. The passage is (sadly) frequent, due to death. A deceased human becomes an invisible; he or she may then lose (because they are denied the possibility of asserting them) their ability to subjectivize themselves, some of their personas, or even their person (by becoming an anonymous ghost).

---

26 The case of fox spirits – the subject of a widespread possession cult that is alive and well in the Chinese world today – is illustrative: in their spiritual progression in contact with humans, they acquire human form and human names. Another case in point is Lüzu's 呂祖 (an immortal and major spirit-writing god) main disciple in the spirit-writing cults, Liu Shouyuan 柳守元, who, as his name suggests, was originally a willow tree.

* conversely, invisible → living, through incarnation (or even reincarnation) or possession.[27] A god who incarnates as a human to preach a message is supposed to retain its previously existing divine persona. Examples abound in China (think of the prophets of the so-called Sectarian traditions since the sixteenth century who present themselves as incarnations of Maitreya or Guanyin, for example) as well as in the Indian, Japanese, and other worlds.

* meme → invisible. A good example of such a change is the fictional character who speaks to fans in their dreams or becomes the object of a possession cult. As a character defined by a closed corpus of images and stories, it is a meme, but when it begins to appear at its own will, it becomes something else. Examples of fictional characters becoming active gods (if this is indeed what happened in chronological order, which is typically difficult to establish beyond doubt) abound in China: the eccentric monk Jigong 濟公 or the Pilgrim Monkey Sun Wukong 孫悟空 are supposed to have been fictional characters before becoming the object of a cult and becoming subjects, through possession and spirit-writing.[28] A human who invents a person (in a role-playing game, video-game, or fiction-writing context) and endows it with one or more personas, cultural conditions permitting, allows this person to take on an existence as an invisible, interact with other persons (human, invisible, or other) and even subjectivize itself. Christophe Pons has analyzed the remarkable case of Fernando Pessoa (1888–1935), who invented several authorial personas, endowing them with their own histories and styles, and maintaining intersubjective relations with them.[29]

* object → invisible. A consecrated or animated object becomes an opaque trace of an invisible entity. The object itself may be visible or hidden. The support of the kami (mirror, other object) in Shinto temples is (with rare exceptions) not visible to anyone, and in many shrines, people who come to pray are unaware of the support they are addressing beyond closed doors and sealed boxes. The consecration of an icon, a mask... is a common ritual device that enables the object to become an invisible (even if it retains its physicality) that can become a person

---

27 In the Chinese context, descriptions of the afterlife take care to describe in great detail how the person about to be reincarnated loses their quality as a person (they are drugged to make them forget everything).

28 Meir Shahar, "Vernacular Fiction and the Transmission of Gods' Cults in Late Imperial China," in *Unruly Gods: Divinity and Society in China*, ed. Meir Shahar & Robert P. Weller (Honolulu: University of Hawai'i Press, 1996), 184–211.

29 Pons, "La possibilité de ne pas être soi."

and even a subject.[30] In the case of consecrated objects that remain visible (such as a statue kept in plain view), we are dealing with entities that find themselves between two modes of existence, combining them or being between them in an indeterminate way, like Schrödinger's cat.

2.2 Change of degree of singularity

An entity can also move forward in the chain entity > agent > individual > person > subject, or backward (I do not focus on backward moves in this short essay). These changes of state, whether incremental or simultaneous, can be perceived and described in two general ways, depending on how we assign agency to humans and non-humans: 1) the entity changes state on its own initiative and by its own means; 2) a ritual device set up by humans enables an entity to enter into relationship with other entities (human or otherwise) and change state. In other words, entities can develop their singularity and gain abilities thanks to humans, or independently of them. I developed a similar typology (revelations decided by the gods vs. ritually arranged by humans) in my book on revelations in China.[31] Each specific combination of these two patterns depends, among other factors, on the regime of evidence operating in the socio-cultural context concerned, notably the regime of evidence for the qualification of invisible entities – that is, what is acceptable as spontaneous divine actions? And as ritually produced ones?

In the first case, we deal with events in which entities manifest themselves spontaneously (i.e., in a way that is perceived as spontaneous), going beyond their assigned role and human expectations, thus overflowing. This notion of overflow is particularly studied by Gregory Delaplace in his comparative study of the self-expressions of the dead.[32] Several anthropologists have taken an interest in these situations, attempting to describe the conditions of possibility of such events, from a pragmatic point of view inspired by William James (1842–1910) among others, for whom it is necessary to base oneself on the observed effects induced by enti-

---

30 Laurel Kendall, *Mediums and Magical Things. Statues, Paintings, and Masks in Asian Places* (Berkeley: University of California Press, 2021). The literature on icons behaving as persons is considerable; see for example Isabelle Charleux, "Miraculous Images of Mongolia from the Sixteenth century to the Present," *Ars Orientalis* 50 (2021): 129–56.

31 Vincent Goossaert, *Making the Gods Speak: The Ritual Production of Revelation in Chinese Religious History* (Cambridge, Mass: Harvard University Asia Center, 2022), chap. 1.

32 Grégory Delaplace, *La voix des fantômes. Quand débordent les morts* (Paris: Seuil, 2024).

ties (invisible or not) and not on a preconceived definition of what these entities are and can do.[33]

In the second case, which has been more studied in the field of history of religions, we are talking about devices that give humans a measure of control over the other, notably invisible, entities with which they wish to enter into relationship – which often does not prevent these invisible entities from overstepping their role. The difference between these two patterns is obviously ideal-typical, as agency is very often shared between humans, invisibles, and others. Events induced by a ritual device favor the occurrence of apparently spontaneous events, and vice versa.

It is important to emphasize that invisible persons can attempt to subjectivize themselves in the absence of any ritual device at their disposal, or in spite of the hostility of the humans concerned to such a prospect, and even in spite of ritual devices designed to prevent the emergence of any invisible subject, which we will come back to in the next section. The emergence of invisible subjects is therefore not simply the mechanical result of ritual procedures. However, it seems clear to me that, in the absence of ritual devices made available to the invisible, these attempts at subjectivation are not fully successful; the Mongolian dead described by Grégory Delaplace, vengeful but present in a place where there are no shamans to let them speak, express their desires and affects through cries or fleeting apparitions, but not through constructed speech.[34] More generally, I know of no case where words revealed by the gods or other invisibles are accepted and circulated in a society where no ritual is practiced that allows the invisibles to express themselves. The case of biblical revelations is no exception: these revelations are given as having taken place in an entirely different society, pre-Christian Hebrew society. In Christian societies, which do not have an accepted ritual mechanism for letting God speak, the divine word can hardly be subjective: inspired people can produce prophecies, which convey information but have no connection with the divine interiority. The Virgin Mary's word, on the other hand, is far more prolix, and enables her to develop a specific persona.[35]

---

33 See in particular the introduction to Ruy Blanes and Diana Espírito Santo, eds., *The Social Life of Spirits* (Chicago: University of Chicago Press, 2013).
34 Delaplace, *La voix des fantômes*.
35 Claverie, *Les guerres de la vierge*. See also a believers' website, reflecting on how Mary's utterances delineate a persona: https://apparitionsdemarie.com/commentaire-sur-les-attitudes-de-la-vierge/

For these reasons, my interest rests primarily in existing ritual devices, i.e. those that are more or less regularly practiced and socially accepted as valid (by at least part of the population) in a given social and cultural context. I propose that, in each context, the repertoire of existing ritual devices for letting persons and subjects emerge strongly conditions the events observed and the field of possibilities for all entities, especially the invisible ones. I therefore propose to sketch out a general repertoire of these devices in order to compare their use or lack thereof between different socio-cultural contexts.

2.3 A repertoire of ritual devices available to the invisible

The following is a non-exhaustive list of the types of ritual devices that enable entities to change state, hopefully conceived in a sufficiently general and open-ended way to be useful for cross-cultural comparison. In most cases, ritual devices are time-bound; they have a beginning (opening up relations between different entities) and an end (closing this space of relations, in order to maintain control).

A. **Naming**. Giving a singular name to an entity can be the object of various forms of institutionalization: any curious or erudite person can propose an identification when an invisible entity manifests itself (orally at the time, in writing in an essay, a commemorative inscription...); granting a title is generally the privilege of a religious and/or political authority.[36] Naming allows an entity to reach the 3–individual level.

B. **Narration**. Telling stories about the entity, its history or qualities, orally or in writing (hymns, plays, songs, novels, epics, chronicles, miracle stories, etc.). Narration enables an entity to reach at least degree 3–individual, usually degree 4–person, and sometimes degree 5–potential (but not actual) subject.

C. **Figuration: creating an effigy** (portrait, statue, mask). Constraints vary from one socio-cultural context to another; sometimes the entity itself plays a role in determining its figurative representation. For example, Chinese gods give self-portraits revealed by spirit-writing; there are also self-revealed icons (skt. *svayambhu*). Figuration enables an entity to reach at least degree 3–individual, and often helps it to reach degree 4–person: it expresses a persona (facial expres-

---

36 For a comparison of procedures for giving titles to Greek and Chinese gods, see Theodora Suk Fong Jim, "Divine Naming in Greek and Chinese Polytheism," in *What's in a Divine Name? Religious Systems and Human Agency in the Ancient Mediterranean*, ed. Alaya Palamidis and Corinne Bonnet (Berlin: De Gruyter, 2024), 59–78.

sion, posture, clothing, and attributes) and enables an interpersonal relationship with the human coming to solicit the effigy.

D. **Animation of a support**: to ritually invite an entity to reside temporarily or permanently in a material object, figurative (portrait, statue, mask...) or not (tablet, mirror, talisman...). Animation enables an entity to reach at least degree 3–individual, and often helps it to reach degree 4–person. The animated support (such as an icon of Guanyin or the Virgin, etc.) is generally considered to be capable of acting and establishing an interpersonal relationship with the human who solicits it.

E. **Invitation**. During a ritual (sacrifice, offering), the officiant (ritual specialist or not) invites (through prayers, invocations, talismans...) entities to be present to receive offerings and listen to prayers, then sends them away. The invitation allows an entity to reach at least degree 3–individual.

F. **Playing** the entity (usually a god) in theater, masked dance, or role-playing. In some cases, the human playing the god is ritually possessed/transformed into the god played. The play or game enables an entity to reach at least degree 4–person, since the entity played shows a persona (the way it behaves, what it says...). When this played god expresses itself, it is a potential subject, or even, if it possesses the actor or player, an actual subject.

G. **Possession**: leaving (voluntarily or involuntarily) the use of one's body (in whole or in part) to an entity so that it can express itself through voice, movement, etc. Possession allows an entity to reach at least degree 3–individual (a spirit identifying itself), often degree 4–person (a spirit asserting its own persona and values), and even degree 5 (when the possessing entity expresses itself as a subject and exposes its affects and ambitions). I place divine utterances commonly referred to as oracles as traces of events enabled by this type of ritual device, even if in many cases of ancient oracles known from transmitted texts, the ritual technique used is not well known (in some cases it can be the product of "artificial," in Cicero's terms, divination without any divine intervention). On the other hand, the fact of writing down and openly disseminating the words of the invisibles produced by possession – this is the case of oracles in Japan, for example – creates a fundamental difference with a possession event that remains oral, not disseminated beyond witnesses other than by hearsay, insofar as written dissemination enables the divine person, or even the divine subject, to be in touch with a large number of persons in other places and times, who were not witnesses to the initial event.

H. **Spirit-writing**: inviting the invisibles to communicate discursive messages through a ritual technique that gives them control over the means of writing. In most contexts, spirit-writing can be considered a special case of possession, but

82 —— Vincent Goossaert

the ritual techniques are specific, as is the mode of expression. Spirit-writing enables an entity to reach at least degree 4–person, but often also degree 5–subject. In
the Chinese context, the texts revealed by spirit-writing, which are widely circulated, include many statements in which the gods talk about themselves, their
history, their affects, their ambitions, and constantly reaffirm their way of being
and their specific style, often without this seeming to serve an informative purpose (as the humans receiving these statements already know this information).[37]

I. **Visualization & shamanism**: creating a mental space where one (or more)
invisible entity is present and can interact with the human practicing visualization or shamanic journeying. Visualization enables an entity to reach at least
degree 3–individual (the visionary or shaman recognizes and names the entities
he or she encounters), often degree 4–person (when the human practitioner and
the visualized entity enter into dialogue), or even degree 5–subject. In some visualization techniques, the practitioner identifies himself with the god (in Chinese,
bianshen 變身 or 變神: "to transform oneself" or "to transform oneself into a
god").

J. **Dreams and journeys** into the other world (in a state of apparent death,
etc.). Dreams, in which we meet and dialogue with the invisible, can be spontaneous, but can also be ritually solicited in various societies (China, Japan, ancient
Greece...).[38] Like visualization, dreaming and other mental experiences enable an
entity to reach at least degree 3–individual, often degree 4–person (when the
human practitioner and the visualized entity enter into dialogue), or even degree
5–subject.

3 The politics of the invisible

Both the occurrence of "spontaneous" events (spirits manifesting themselves un-
invited, as far as we know) and the deployment of ritual devices to enable invisibles to form relationships, and humans to control them, are conditioned by (culturally specific) cognitive and technological frameworks: not all ritual techniques
attested in human history are known to everyone everywhere. But they are also

---

37 I insist on this "self-performance" dimension of the spirit-writing gods in Vincent Goossaert,
"Learning with the Gods in China, 1600-1900" (forthcoming).
38 Yang Qin, "Ritual Production of Divine Dreams in Ancient Greece and Early Modern China"
(under review).

constrained by reasoned choices, and therefore of a political nature: not everything that is cognitively and technically possible is politically acceptable, and most cultures place limits on the possibilities of action available to various types of entities, including the invisibles. First and foremost, these cultures limit the access of the invisibles to the status of person and, more specifically, subject.

The case of possession is obviously emblematic; in most cultures, even those where possession remains very commonly and publicly practiced – as in the Chinese, Japanese, Indian, African, and other worlds – it is the subject of statements and measures aimed at limiting its capacity to let all kinds of entities subjectify themselves. Since the end of the nineteenth century, these measures have been reinforced by the campaigns against "superstitions" that have marked all these cultural areas, but they predate them.[39]

In the case of China (and others), the prohibitions against possession (which are hardly fully respected) are partly linked to a fear of the political prophecies that can be expressed, but more broadly reflect a mistrust of what entities not recognized by the state – and even those that are recognized but which people in power wish to control – can do and say. More broadly, despite the wide range of ritual devices that have long been well known, successive Chinese regimes since the beginning of our era have tried to limit their use. Possession, as well as spirit-writing, is forbidden in the imperial code of the Ming (1368–1644) and Qing (1636–1911). What is more, many gods, though recognized and worshipped by the imperial state, were denied personhood. To take a striking example, at the beginning of the Ming dynasty, the City gods (Chenghuangshen 城隍神) became the object of official worship in each administrative seat, but the imperial state very quickly imposed an identity for the god as generic, not personal (no proper name and no birthday), even though the people (and even the officials in charge of worship) venerated them as deceased historical persons with a persona of their own.[40] Another measure inspired by comparable concerns is the Qing emperors' ban (also little respected) on impersonating the god Guandi on stage.[41]

---

39 For the Chinese case, Vincent Goossaert & David A. Palmer, *The Religious Question in Modern China* (Chicago: University of Chicago Press, 2011).

40 Vincent Goossaert, "Managing Chinese Religious Pluralism in the Nineteenth-century City Gods Temples," in *Globalization and the Making of Religious Modernity in China*, ed. Thomas Jansen, Thoralf Klein, Christian Meyer (Boston, Brill, 2014), 29–51.

41 Wu Zhen 吴真, "Jingji, hangdang, juchang: jindai xiqu de fei wenxue yanjin jizhi" 禁忌、行当、剧场：近代戏曲的非文学演进机制, *Wenyi yanjiu* 文艺研究 1 (2022): 124–36.

One form of control exercised over possession by politico-religious institutions is the dissemination of the idea that the great gods, with their universal powers, do not possess mediums (for reasons of purity or dignity). Possession can only concern inferior spirits, who can, in the best of cases, bring benefits or useful information, but who should also be handled with care, and who are themselves under the authority of the higher gods. This is the case, for example, in Hindu traditions[42] ; similarly, Buddhist traditions admit possession by gods, but not – in theory – by Buddhas and bodhisattvas. In China, however, gods who are not at the very top of the divine hierarchy but nevertheless play the role of universal saviors, such as Guandi, Lüzu 呂祖, or Wenchang 文昌, are highly subjectivized and maintain dense intersubjective relationships with humans.[43]

Furthermore, the groups that provide the gods with the ritual devices that enable them to subjectify themselves do not all have the same degree of tolerance towards invisible subjects. In the revelations produced by some groups, the gods say "I" essentially to set an example of moral rules. In other corpuses of spirit-writing revelations, on the other hand, the overflow and expression of affect is much more present, even from the same gods as in the cases mentioned just above. The censorship is not explicit, but its effect is in quite plain view when we compare what a same god says in different places.

Another way of controlling the emergence of invisible subjects is to confine them to an elsewhere, either temporal or spatial. Japanese myths have the kami speak as subjects, but in the "age of gods," succeeded by the "age of men," their descendants, in which we now live; the gods remain active and give oracles, but these oracles are more rarely the expression of divine subjects. In the same way, the great Hindu gods (Visnu, Siva, Devi) speak for themselves in mythical texts (such as the *Puranas*) but are not supposed to possess mediums today. The situation in ancient Greece is quite comparable with divine subjects more vibrantly expressed in myths than in cults (gods in Homer are scripted yet exuberant subjects). There were recorded oracles where the gods spoke (even though we know nothing about the ritual techniques that produced them), but the questions were framed in a way not conducive to subjectivation: the gods were required to pro-

---

42 Reiniche, "Un nom, une forme, un lieu"; Fuller, *The Camphor Flame*, chapter 2, "Gods and Goddesses."

43 Goossaert, *Making the Gods Speak*.

vide help and information but not asked what they thought. Similarly, epiphanies, although numerous, were rarely occasions for subjectivation.[44]

4 Comparative overtures

In order to test the heuristic validity of the avenues outlined above, I would like to develop a comparative approach, as open as possible, even if my personal interests and collaborations lead me first to certain privileged comparenda: ancient Greece; Japan; premodern and modern Hindu traditions; Mongolia; and Catholic Europe. In these cases, and in all the others to which the comparison will open, I wish to ask the following questions: what is the availability, on the one hand, and the political and cultural acceptance, on the other, of the various ritual devices that enable the emergence of invisible persons and subjects? More specifically, can people, and how can people, have recourse to the five types of ritual devices that seem to me to be at the heart of subjectivation processes: Performance (theater, role-playing...); Possession; Spirit-writing; Visualizations and shamanism; and Dreams and visits to the other world? What cultures and religious traditions enable the production and reception of the gods' discourse on themselves through these five means? More specifically, what are the conditions of possibility for the autobiographies of the gods, which are a particularly strong and public form of expression of divine subjectivity? Chinese religious traditions have produced a good number of these autobiographies, in particular by spirit-writing[45] ; what might be comparable productions in other religious contexts, and what are their conditions of possibility?

To kick off the discussion, let us say a few more words about ancient Greece, continuing the comparison initiated above, based on my limited readings and discussions with colleagues in Greek studies, especially Theodora Jim and Gabriella Pironti. Performance existed in Greece, the gods were sometimes present on stage, and might even bless the audience – but their speech was rare and totally scripted, as far as we know (obviously, we mostly have the scripts). Possession may have existed, but is nowhere clearly described, and the mode of production

---

44 Georgia Petridou, *Divine Epiphany in Greek Literature and Culture* (Oxford: Oxford University Press, 2016).
45 For Wenchang's autohagiography, see Terry F. Kleeman, *A God's Own Tale. The Book of Transformations of Wenchang, the Divine Lord of Zitong* (Albany: State University of New York Press, 1994).

of oracles remains largely unknown. In the latter, the gods may occasionally speak in the first person, but speak little of themselves. Spirit-writing and visualization, as far as we know, are not documented. Dreams were often recorded, even ritually solicited, and allowed interpersonal contact with the gods to request a favor or information. The intersubjective relationship between human and god, on the other hand, is rarely evoked, and in Euripides' play *Hippolytus* – where the hero has an intense, shared affective relationship with the goddess Artemis –, this is described as dangerous and strongly discouraged: the hero ends up tragically. Here, then, we have a very significant presence of divine persons, whose stories are told in all kinds of genres – from the point of view of personalization, comparisons with the Chinese case and others are eminently possible and fruitful. In ancient Greece, on the other hand, there is almost no well-documented possibility of subjectivation, both because of the lack of ritual techniques available and the judgments made about their use. Divine subjectivation may have existed in ancient Greece, but it remains a significant fact that we have no clear record of it, by contrast to premodern and modern China, where it is overabundant.

References

Blanes, Ruy, and Diana Espírito Santo, eds. *The Social Life of Spirits*. Chicago: University of Chicago Press, 2013.
Bouchy, Anne. *Les oracles de Shirataka: vie d'une femme spécialiste de la possession dans le Japon du XXe siècle*. Toulouse: Presses Universitaires du Mirail, 2005.
Charleux, Isabelle. "Miraculous Images of Mongolia from the Sixteenth century to the Present." *Ars Orientalis* 50 (2021): 129–56.
Claverie, Elisabeth. *Les guerres de la Vierge. Une anthropologie des apparitions*. Paris: Gallimard, 2003.
Dawkins, Richard. *The Selfish Gene*. Oxford: Oxford University Press, 1976.
De Antoni, Andrea, "Steps to an Ecology of Spirits. Comparing Feelings of More-than-Human, Immaterial Meshworks?" *More-than-Human Worlds: A NatureCulture Blog Series*, https://www.natcult.net/steps-to-an-ecology-of-spirits/
De Antoni, Andrea, "Affect." In *The International Encyclopedia of Anthropology*, edited by Hilary Callan. Hoboken: John Wiley & Sons, 2020.
Delaplace, Grégory. *La voix des fantômes. Quand débordent les morts*. Paris: Seuil, 2024.
Delaplace, Grégory. "Introduction. L'invisible tel qu'il apparaît." *Ateliers d'anthropologie* 52 (2022).
Fuller, Christopher John. *The Camphor Flame: Popular Hinduism and Society in India*. Princeton: Princeton University Press, 2004.
Goossaert, Vincent. "Learning with the Gods in China, 1600–1900," forthcoming.
Goossaert, Vincent. *Making the Gods Speak: The Ritual Production of Revelation in Chinese Religious History*. Cambridge, Mass: Harvard University Asia Center, 2022.

Goossaert, Vincent. "Managing Chinese Religious Pluralism in the Nineteenth-century City Gods Temples." In *Globalization and the Making of Religious Modernity in China*, edited by Thomas Jansen, Thoralf Klein, Christian Meyer, 29–51. Boston, Brill, 2014.

Goossaert, Vincent. "The Social Networks of Gods in Late Imperial Spirit-writing Altars." *Religions* 14.2, 217 (2023) https://doi.org/10.3390/rel14020217.

Goossaert, Vincent. "Petits dieux chinois." In *Entre évitement et alliance, Formes mineures du divin*, edited by Jean-Pierre Albert and Agnes Kedzierska Manzon. Turnhout: Brepols, 2024, pp. 77–92.

Goossaert, Vincent. "Ritual Techniques for Creating a Divine Persona in Late Imperial China: The Case of Daoist Law Enforcer Lord Wang." *Journal of Chinese Religions* 50 (2022): 45–76.

Goossaert, Vincent & David A. Palmer. *The Religious Question in Modern China*. Chicago: University of Chicago Press, 2011.

Jim, Theodora Suk Fong, "Divine Naming in Greek and Chinese Polytheism." In *What's in a Divine Name? Religious Systems and Human Agency in the Ancient Mediterranean*, edited by Alaya Palamidis and Corinne Bonnet, 59–78. Berlin: De Gruyter, 2024.

Kendall, Laurel. Mediums and Magical Things. Statues, Paintings, and Masks in Asian Places. Berkeley: University of California Press, 2021.

Kleeman, Terry F. *A God's Own Tale. The Book of Transformations of Wenchang, the Divine Lord of Zitong*. Albany: State University of New York Press, 1994.

Luhrmann, Tanya M. *How God Becomes Real: Kindling the Presence of Invisible Others*. Princeton: Princeton University Press, 2020.

Naquin, Susan. *Gods of Mount Tai: Familiarity and the Material Culture of North China, 1000–2000*. Leiden: Brill, 2022.

Petridou, Georgia. *Divine Epiphany in Greek Literature and Culture*. Oxford: Oxford University Press, 2016.

Piette, Albert. "L'entité jusqu'au bout. À propos de la question ontologique en anthropologie." *Religiologiques: sciences humaines et religion* 43 (2022): 91–111.

Pirenne-Delforge, Vinciane and Gabriella Pironti. "Many vs. One." In *The Oxford Handbook of Ancient Greek Religion*, edited by Esther Eidinow & Julia Kindt, 39–47. Oxford: Oxford University Press, 2015.

Pons, Christophe. "La possibilité de ne pas être soi. Sujet, spiritisme et libre-arbitre au Portugal." *Journal des anthropologues* 164–165 (2021): 111–29.

Pratchett, Terry. *Small Gods*. London: Victor Gollancz, 1992.

Reiniche, Marie-Louise. "Un nom, une forme, un lieu: L'invention hindoue de l'autre et du même." *Revue de l'histoire des religions* 205.4 (1988): 367–83.

Sahlins, Marshall. "Cosmic Economics." *Annals of the Fondazione Luigi Einaudi* 55 (2021): 255–78.

Shahar, Meir. "Vernacular Fiction and the Transmission of Gods' Cults in Late Imperial China." In *Unruly Gods: Divinity and Society in China*, edited by Meir Shahar & Robert P. Weller, 184–211. Honolulu: University of Hawai'i Press, 1996.

Souriau, Étienne. *Les différents modes d'existence: Suivi de "Du mode d'existence de l'œuvre à faire"*. *Présentation par Isabelle Stengers et Bruno Latour*. Paris: Puf, 2015.

Ter Haar, Barend. *Guan Yu: the Religious Afterlife of a Failed Hero*. Oxford: Oxford University Press, 2017.

Vernant, Jean-Pierre. *Mythe et pensée chez les Grecs*, Études de psychologie historique. Paris: Maspero, 1965.

Versnel, Hendrik Simon. *Coping with the Gods*. Leiden: Brill, 2011.

Wu Zhen 吴真. "Jingji, hangdang, juchang: jindai xiqu de fei wenxue yanjin jizhi" 禁忌、行当、剧场：近代戏曲的非文学演进机制, *Wenyi yanjiu* 文艺研究 1 (2022): 124–36.

Yang, Qin. "Ritual Production of Divine Dreams in Ancient Greece and Early Modern China," under review.

Yü, Chün-fang. *Kuan-yin: the Chinese Transformation of Avalokitesvara*. New York: Columbia University Press, 2001.

www.ingramcontent.com/pod-product-compliance
Lightning Source LLC
Jackson TN
JSHW021610260625
86719JS00006B/23